Pr
College Su

MW00622635

"College Success for Moms is written by a woman who writes from her own life experience. Dianna Blake writes for women who are moms, looking to better their lives through education. I'm inspired by Dianna's words and advice. She encourages moms to believe in themselves and begin the journey of education. Being a mom and working toward a better future by attending college is not easy; having this guide book will help you stay on the path to self-confidence and life fulfillment. This is a much needed resource for women choosing to better their lives through education, while continuing to be good mothers and role models to their children." –Patricia Peters Martin, Ph.D., clinical psychologist and author of *The Other Couch: Discovering Women's Wisdom in Therapy and Liars, Cheats, and Creeps: Leaving the Sociopath Behind.*

"Finally, a college success book written for moms by a mom! This book is a revelation. The information is expert but is shared in a way that makes you feel like you're in a living room with close friends. Dianna's personal story is gut-wrenching and deeply inspiring. No mom should do college alone and Dianna is the perfect mentor." –Is Adney, M.Ed, student life professional and author of *Community College Success: How to Finish with Friends, Scholarships, Internships, and the Career of Your Dreams*

College Success for Moms

*How to Finish with
Confidence and a Bright Future
While Raising Your Family*

by

Dianna Blake, B.A.

Printed in the United States of America
ISBN: 978-0-9976834-2-4

Book design by Sammie and Vorris Dee Justesen
Cover design by Praditha Kahatapitiya

First printing, 2016

Dedication

For my children, husband, mom, and my angel of a grandmother.

This book is also dedicated to every mother who has gone through (or is considering) college, whether you are single, married, widowed, pregnant, or the mother of one child or many. Each one of you has the ability to succeed.

College Success for Moms
Table of Contents

Introduction

My Story

A DECADE AGO, I was nobody. That's how I felt about myself, because I wasn't educated, driven, or passionate about anything. I saw nothing in my future besides caring for my two children, Matthew and Sarah, and I thought I'd never be able to make their lives turn out better than my own. I had basically given up on myself and my family.

Ten years before that, I was stuck on the idea finding the right guy would make me happy through marriage and children. I had already walked away from friends, family, church, and the few modest goals I set for myself, always in search of approval from a man. As the only child of a single, disabled mother (with autism-like symptoms) who worked a low-wage job, I had no positive role model for furthering my education. To compensate for the absence of a father, I learned to seek love and approval from the wrong people.

When it was time to consider college I was already working full-time at a fast food restaurant while living with a boyfriend. The guy of my dreams was ambitious, but only concerning his own desires. I lost myself and spent time going into debt and burning bridges I would later regret. Instead of "happily ever after," our relationship ended and I ran away. I am a runner—or used to be. When troubles piled up, instead of facing them I went looking for greener pastures somewhere else.

Over the course of ten years I became a single mom, attempting community college once, but giving up when I felt like an outcast. I spent time searching for happiness and purpose in the wrong places. I also spent time in denial, as I knew my son had developmental delays that shouldn't be ignored. Finally, when my first child was three, I met my husband David. We would have a little girl right before he lost his job and I spiraled into postpartum depression so terrible that, once again, I ran—this time with two young children.

One night when the kids were in bed asleep and I lay sweating and drunk on a cold basement floor in Massachusetts, I realized how badly I'd messed up. It took hitting rock bottom, missing my grandmother's memorial, and turning my back on family to change me. I knew that somehow I had to make things right. I needed to finally "be the change" I wanted to see in my own life. It was time for me to grow up and do better for my children.

So I went home. I worked on my marriage. I gave birth to another son. And I enrolled full-time in college after his first birthday. To my surprise, I succeeded, earning a 4.0 GPA for the first year and close to that marker for the second year. I consecutively won a place on the President's List and people recommended me for jobs and special events. After I won the Phi Theta Kappa All-California Academic Team Award, my confidence soared and I realized I could do anything if I stuck to it. So, I applied to be a member of the Pearson Student Advisory Board.

When I first walked into the Pearson Student Leadership Summit in July 2013, I never expected to leave with a plan far bigger than my assignment as an advisory board member. Yet, my life changed when our group did an exercise where each person talked about her past, present, and future. I felt a bit awkward in this group because I was an older mom in college, but that same attribute pushed me toward a surprising goal. You see, I entered the room as Dianna: mother, wife, and English major. I left the room with all those things intact, but I also began viewing myself as a mentor, a writer, and a motivational speaker who could inspire mothers to value themselves and reach their full potential as college students.

Where did those ideas come from? I realized they'd been growing inside me during the entire time I worked my way through college. I believe every step of the journey brought me to that moment of realization.

After the summit, I wasted no time setting up a blog called College Success for Moms, because I felt compelled to connect with moms who were either in college or considering that option. I knew these women needed a voice; someone who could help them. I knew this because I struggled through college without a role model for balancing school and family obligations.

The number of student-parents grows larger every year, and the majority of these students are women. Yet, many campuses are not mom-friendly when it comes to college success. Others offer helpful programs, but many students don't know how to find the support they need. I wanted my blog to reach these frustrated women and help them not only survive college, but thrive and succeed.

My blog had a slow first year, with only five thousand views. However, my readership grew as I wrote more consistently. Halfway through the second year I hit ten thousand readers. Now, after three years, I have over 60,000 views—a milestone I never imagined. Not only did my readership grow, but readers began sharing my posts. Despite my self-doubt, other women responded to the diary entries, personal stories from other moms, advice, and information on my blog. Making personal connections with other moms in college was a huge bonus. Over the last two years I've met nearly a dozen mothers from different backgrounds who attend college all over the United States. They opened my eyes to the diversity of this audience and their experiences. I learned the college experience is vastly different for women with children; more complicated than it is for men with children and students with no children.

While writing the blog I searched for books that would help mothers like myself, but came up empty handed. I found nothing written by a mom in college for other moms in college. And that's how this journey began.

Dianna Blake

Chapter 1

Believe in Yourself

CHARLENE

"I didn't fail because I didn't give up. My advice to you is: Don't give up. You will stumble, you will fall, and you'll sometimes feel it's too hard to stay on this path. Don't give in to what is easy. You only fail if you stop trying. The look on your children's faces and the pride you feel will make all your struggles worthwhile in the end."

WHEN I FIRST started attending Mt. San Antonio College, I didn't believe I could succeed as a student. In fact, I didn't even know why I'd enrolled. Fortunately, my attitude began to change over time. After surviving one semester, I believed I could do it again, and again. Along with the struggle to balance school and family life, I also dealt with self-doubt, not-so-perfect class experiences, employment issues, and feeling alone. I desperately needed a book like this one to bolster my confidence.

I'd like you to bookmark this page right now, because believing you can succeed is half the battle. When doubts arise (and they will), read this chapter again.

Self-Doubt

Most of my issues in college stemmed from the lack of confidence that haunted me since my formative years in elementary school. During these awkward years I was just average: my clothes, hair, number of friends, and grades—all average (if not below). I had friends, but they were outcasts. While I'm proud to say I was friends with the friendless, it hurts to look back and think about how other students treated me. Like the outcasts, I was friendless at one point. My clothes were average because I came from a low-income family and wore what I was given. My hair? Well, my mom enjoyed having it cut short because she liked hers short. She didn't know what it did to me on an emotional level because, as a grown woman who coped with an intellectual disability her entire life, she couldn't relate to me on a social level. She didn't know I spent half of sixth grade being called Bobby Brady and getting teased about my clothes. These factors distracted me in school because I always worried about being bullied. Therefore, my grades suffered. Yet, I did like school for a while—until fourth grade. That year, when a teacher called me stupid in front of the class, I erected a wall around myself. I didn't want to be humiliated ever again, so I stopped trying.

In spite of all that baggage, I pulled myself together and graduated from college. Now, my self-confidence continues to grow, and although I still doubt myself at times, I *know* I'm capable of succeeding.

I am here.

I am capable.

I will succeed, in spite of all odds.

If you can look past your own self-doubts, you are already halfway to success in college.

Changing Your Self Talk

If you lack confidence, you won't be able to reach a self-assured mindset right away, but you can take the first step NOW by changing your self-talk. You must believe you can be successful in order for it to happen. So how can you go from insecure student to confident scholar? Many chapters in this book focus on helping with this journey, but we'll begin with several concepts that inspired me to overcome fear and insecurity when I entered college:

Acknowledge your feelings. For me, the first step toward overcoming self-doubt was to recognize my negative feelings and acknowledge that I needed an attitude change. For a long time I tried to deny self-doubt by projecting it onto the people around me. I didn't have a problem—they did. I convinced myself that having other people doubt my abilities caused me to give up and fail.

Once I recognized my insecurities and the need to face them, I could accept the fact that I'd be dealing with complex emotions over being a student. These feelings may include guilt, intimidation, fear, and anxiety, to name a few. This knowledge gave me the security to deal with problems one at a time. If you can acknowledge your own self-doubt (even going so far as to say it out loud), then you can overcome these self-imposed obstacles.

Keep a journal. At least once a week I would write in a journal, but during moments of self-doubt I grabbed that spiral-bound book and jotted down all my thoughts and feelings. By doing this, I often felt as though I purged negativity from my mind.

Have a set of mantras on hand. When you start telling yourself you're going to fail, you're a bad mom, and college is way too hard, that's the time to fight back with mantras— positive things you recite aloud to yourself and write in your journal. These might include:

I can succeed.

I will get through this.

I am a great mom AND a good student.

These mantras helped me through difficult times over the course of my education and I still use them when self-doubt rears its ugly head. Find mantras that work for you and, when you start telling yourself ugly things, fight back with these phrases. If you don't know where to begin, think about your favorite songs. Offhand I know quite a few empowerment songs especially for women. If you enjoy music, songs may be the place to seek out your own set of mantras.

Don't compare yourself to others. I cannot tell you how many times I've caught myself making comparisons between my work and what everyone else is doing. This is not healthy for many reasons, most importantly because we're all on our own journeys and we each face different challenges. As someone who is balancing school with parenting, and possibly a job as well, you have so much on your plate. It makes no sense to compare your situation to people who seem to have it all together. They might be okay in one area, but what else is going on in their lives? Sure they joined three clubs, went to all the school events, held an academic internship, and stayed active in sports; did they do this all with a child or children? My guess is those people aren't trying to raise children while also attempting to finish college. When you find yourself comparing, look back to the person you were five weeks, five months, or even five years ago. Are you proud of your accomplishments? If not, then you can analyze ways to improve, based on your own experiences.

Hang a timeline board near your study space at home. This is different than a vision board, which mostly focuses on the future. A timeline board is a way to acknowledge and respect your past, notice your present experiences, and plan for the future. I suggest keeping a timeline of your life experiences — good and not-so-good. As you hit a milestone, add it to the timeline. You will begin to see a string of moments where you overcame difficulties or were rewarded for your hard work. This visual representation of your success might be the key to believing yourself capable.

Surround yourself with positive people. When I look back over the last few years, positive people in my life are what I appreciate most. These people range from classmates to professors, and church members. Their confidence in me truly lifted me up during the most doubtful moments of my education. During the semester where my husband nearly died from a major illness, my church family pulled together and helped out through meals, financial donations, and constant kindness in the form of words of affirmation. If you don't attend church, that's okay—seek out the helpers and the dreamers. Look for people like yourself who want to succeed, and you too will believe you can.

The Critics

Have you met the mom-shamers? These critics can be other women, other students, your family, or random people who bombard you with opinions:

"Your children need you at home!"

"Won't you miss out on your children's lives?

"Why not wait until the children are grown? You're being selfish."

"What will you do when the kids are sick? You'll end up having to drop out."

And so it goes. Why do these people criticize? My only conclusion is that being a mom in college, while becoming more common, is still a non-traditional route for women. Because of this, people will judge you based on their own values and beliefs. This can be linked to the idea of the nuclear family in traditional society: A mom, a dad, 2.5 kids, and a dog. Mom stays home all day and cares for the children and house while dad works full-time. Now, I'm not against this type of family, but the truth is, not many families can manage that ideal. Instead, some men are stay at home dads and millions of women work fulltime. Yet, these old values continue haunting college moms.

YOU are the only one who can make these choices for your life, based on personal values and your own way of doing things. Being a mother has no set job description outside of "love your children." There is no single right way to raise a child, and many paths lead to happy, healthy children.

Never let anyone say you're harming your children by attending college. Actually, you're doing your best to make a better future. You are improving yourself in order to improve their lives. You are setting a wonderful example for your children—an example most children in traditional homes never get to see. The critics will talk (trust me, I know), but consider how many times movie critics bashed a movie you ended up loving. It's the same thing. These people have never walked in your shoes. Don't add to your baggage by criticizing yourself or believing the negative things people say.

Have you noticed that, if ten people praise you for going to school and one person makes a snarky comment, you'll end of thinking only about the negative? That's human nature. Studies show it takes about five positive events to make up for one negative event. The antidote to criticism is letting go of your negative emotions, like anger and self-doubt, and focus on where you're going. Forget the nay-sayers and keep moving forward.

The best way to respond to a critic is by saying something like this: "Thanks for your input, but I'm making the choices I believe are right for me and my family. Perhaps you'll attend my graduation."

The Bad with the Good

Not every class you take in college will be great. Although you may have the highest expectations of your professors, they are human. I could have given up SO many times because of terrible class experiences, but what good would that do? I would only hurt myself by quitting. Did you love all your teachers in high school? Probably not, and college is the same in many ways.

One of my most vivid memories happened during my sophomore year at a community college. During a child development class with one of my favorite professors, the professor grew irritated by the questions students threw at him after our first exam. He went on to give a lecture, and during that lecture I made a comment I felt was relevant. He responded by saying, "That is off topic, Dianna. You do that all the time."

He was offensive to me, and all I could do was look down at my desk and silently cry. At break time the girl in front of me asked if I was okay. I said, "No, I'm not." I walked out of that class and never wanted to return. Not only did the professor humiliate me, he was also wrong. He felt frustrated with the entire class and took out his anger on me. Had he been just another professor I would've felt less wounded, but I truly admired and respected this man. After talking with other professors, I decided to think for a while and then e-mail the professor once I felt calmer. I did this, and he replied with an apology. He later emailed with a more in-depth apology. In fact, he offered to apologize to me in front of the class, but that wasn't necessary. I did return to class and the rest of the semester went well.

What if I hadn't followed up with him? What if I let this one event defeat me? I truly believe I would have dropped out of college. I know you will have incidents like this, plus other negative experiences. There will be humiliating situations, lower grades than you expected, boring classes, snobbish and irritating classmates, mistakes, and misunderstandings. Don't let these things deter you from reaching your goals. Learn from your mistakes, forgive others, and keep your focus on that college degree.

Now that I've told an ugly story (and I only experienced a few), I'll share one of the good times. Yes, the previous story ended well, but it's a memory I would rather not leave you with. One of my fondest memories involves a dreaded class: Speech!

As advised by my counselor, I chose to do the class in an eight-week session in order to get it over with quickly. Now I wish I'd taken the 16-week class so I could learn more, but I'm also thankful I chose this time and professor. The speech class had a positive impact on my life in two ways. First, I formed lasting friendships with at least two of my classmates. I never expected this to happen. I thought I would completely embarrass myself and hide in a corner. Instead, our entire class bonded over our mutual fear of public speaking. Furthermore, we encouraged one another before and after every single speech. What started as the most-dreaded course ended up being a favorite class. I especially liked the diversity in our group.

The second event occurred during my informative speech when I spoke about an important figure in African American (and U.S.) literature. This experience cemented my belief that teaching was my true calling. I had doubted this career choice for so long, but after I finished my speech and people told me they felt like they'd been taught by a professional, I was overwhelmed with happiness. Having the chance to teach others about something I loved was the best!

Unexpected achievements like this one await you in college—and they are golden tickets to your future.

You Are Not Alone

While I understand that at one point or another all students feel alone on their academic journeys, I believe this happens more often for moms in college. Most of the time I was too busy to notice this feeling, but every once in a while I couldn't ignore the loneliness that accompanied being a nontraditional student. In the honors program I was one of the only nontraditional students. As a student advisor with Pearson I was the only college mom; and even as a tutor at my university writing center I was one of the few tutors who had children—and the only one with four kids. I couldn't hide being a mom, nor would I even try, but fitting in would have felt nice.

You'll attend classes with students who don't have to worry about childcare, cooking dinner, and staying up all night with a sick toddler or a teething baby. You may feel isolated and lonely as you listen to chatter about dating, parties, and weekend getaways. When it comes down to it, you may find it hard to strike up a conversation with your peers, and since you probably can't attend a multitude of events, you end up being an outsider. To be honest, I've even felt this way around other moms in college who were much younger than me or had fewer children. They still had the desire to hang out with friends, when all I wanted to do was go home, be with my kids, and sleep. It's not their fault or yours—that's just how it is. I want to tell you how I got through this sense of loneliness during my college career.

I educated myself about the college population. Are you and I actually alone? By the numbers, no. Many moms are attending college and the number grows every year as women reenter the workforce in order to support their families. Thousands of moms (and dads) just like you are trying to succeed in college while raising a family. In 2014, the Institute for Women's Policy Research found that 26% of undergraduate students are parents. Of that number, 71% are mothers. Whatever you're going through, others parents feel the same way. You may not run into many moms in college, but that doesn't mean they aren't there. To further educate yourself, you can visit helpful centers like the re-entry or transfer centers (we will talk about those later).

I focused on my goals. Yes, making friends is great and we'll discuss that later in the book. However, I ultimately overcame feelings of loneliness by remembering why I was there: I wanted an education and I wanted to increase my chances for gaining a career with a livable wage while also improving myself. I wanted to give my children a better life than I had. If I happened to make friends along the way, bonus! So, when I really start feeling isolated and alone, I reassess my situation, write out my plan to graduate (yes, I re-write it), and keep that plan in a place I can constantly see it.

I spent more time with my children. Motherhood is a lonely role for many women. Even though we may be surrounded by small people all day, every day, we crave time with other adults. I agree and acknowledge I've also felt that way. However, when I felt lonely after spending a day on campus or when I was stuck doing homework for hours, I stopped and spent time with my children.

I made a commitment to spend time with mom-in-college friends. At least once a month, I would commit myself to have lunch or dinner with one of my mom-friends in order to catch up. I've always enjoyed these times because we get to set aside our homework and other responsibilities for a brief time and just relax, while chatting over food. I also tried to meet and connect with other moms in college through the re-entry center. I made a few good friends this way and it definitely helped me feel less alone on the journey.

Don't let feelings like loneliness and isolation stop you from succeeding; these experiences will shape you into an excellent job candidate, demonstrating your grit. And if nothing else works, remember that your college education won't last forever.

Don't Let Failure Stop You

Fear of failure is one of the many issues that kept me from believing I could succeed in college. I've failed many, many times at various things, and each time I doubted my ability to move past it. This was especially true during the first few years of school when I had to tackle math and science, both important subjects, but not especially interesting to me. I was hard on myself when I received a C in pre-algebra—a passing grade, but one I felt signified my failure as a student. Even though I made plenty of C's and below during grade school and high school, I hated myself for getting one in college. However, a professor told me straight: "You didn't fail– you earned a C, and that grade represents an average understanding. Also, it's a passing grade."

After that, I learned to feel proud of myself for earning a C in a subject I'd never done well in. The same thing happened in science, except I actually loved the class. Yet, I still couldn't master all the key terms and definitions, so I walked away with a C. After that experience I realized that sometimes earning a B or C actually correlated with how much information I retained. I hadn't failed at all.

The same can be said for having to withdraw from a class. While you should avoid accumulating too many W's on your transcript, a W is a far better grade than an F and it is NOT failing—it shows you were smart enough to know you couldn't move forward successfully for any number of reasons. It's saying "I'm not ready for this" and walking away with your GPA (grade point average) still in one piece. Don't feel you've failed if you come to this realization. You just weren't ready at the time to take that specific class.

If you do fail, don't count yourself out just yet. Believe you can overcome that obstacle and learn from your errors. Nothing is a failure if we learn something valuable from it. Remember that.

You can do this, but perhaps not all at once. As you dive into the rest of this book, keep believing in yourself, but don't try to follow all the advice I give you at once. Yes, I believe it's useful, but I want you to remember that it took me a few years to figure out this whole college thing. Allow yourself time. Take a class. Take a break. Take another class. Join a club. Now, I know you can do it, so let's get started...

Chapter 2

Choose the Best School for You

L<small>IZ</small>

> *"Getting through college takes hard work and dedication, especially as a mom, and I certainly can't take full credit for my achievements. In large part, my success as a returning student was due to the programs and resources in place at my community college. Campus resources completely changed the game for me."*

COLLEGE WASN'T ON my to-do list after graduating high school. I had a great-aunt who encouraged me to continue my education, but she passed away. When I finally decided to pursue a college education at age 21, I enrolled in community college, but soon became pregnant with my first child and dropped out. Something happened to me at that point. I didn't think I could succeed in college and I somehow felt I had no right to attend classes. With that mindset, but still having the desire to learn (and needing a career), I was pulled into some dubious learn-at-home programs. I quickly lost all hope of succeeding in those programs because I had no support from the company and no peers. One after another I started classes and then quit, trailing debt with me along the way simply because I signed up.

I considered a career college at one point, but after five years of failing and/or quitting, I didn't think I could face a classroom. I felt everyone would somehow recognize me as a failure, a drop out. Finally, my husband David recommended I attend Mount San Antonio College near our home—a school he attended and enjoyed. This college gave me an opportunity to learn and recognized my hard work. There, I found the strength to forgive myself for all the times I quit and then prove to myself I wasn't a quitter after all.

You might already be in college, or perhaps you've just selected your school. If so, you can move past this chapter. Choosing the right college is nearly as stressful as being a student, because you'll find so many options to choose from, including community colleges, universities, for profit, and private schools. What are your best options? How do you know which to choose?

As you begin your quest, I recommend consulting with The College Board online, a not-for-profit organization that connects students to colleges (https://www.collegeboard.org/). They offer a step-by-step college search process, plus many other resources.

Be a wise consumer and ask questions about each college you consider:

1. Do credits from this school readily transfer to other colleges and universities?
2. What grades do I need to earn in order to transfer my credit to other colleges?
3. What is the graduation rate for students enrolled at this school?
4. How does the school assist students in finding employment after graduation?
5. What are tuition costs and how do they compare to other schools? (You will find a huge difference from one state to another).
6. How much of the coursework is available through distance learning (online)?
7. Do the degrees offered and courses in the catalog fit the major subject I want to study?

Community College

As a community college graduate, I highly recommend these schools. Many of you want to attend a university, but if you've been out of school for a while, don't have the best academic record, and you're a mother, you should consider starting with community college. Here you can test the waters, taking one or two classes as you get used to being a student. More importantly, community colleges are more likely to welcome mothers, and that means you'll find women like yourself who will support you. Community colleges are more cost-efficient than universities, which is a great benefit if you're low income or haven't decided on a career choice. The cost of community college (in comparison to university fees), allows you to take extra classes in order to find the best career path. Despite what some people say about the community college system, the courses are just as rigorous as a university. In fact, some university professors also teach at local community colleges. I can honestly say my community college professors prepared me to learn at the university level.

University

If you decide to begin your college career at a university, a state university may be the wiser choice, especially as a mom in college. I earned my Bachelor of Arts in English from a state college, even though I had an opportunity to attend a more prestigious private school. I can't say I regret this choice. The university experience varies from on college to another, but for the most part is similar to a community college as far as registration, schedules, and interaction with professors. I was worried that my university professors wouldn't be as accessible as their community college counterparts, but I was wrong. I received just as much, if not more, support from my university professors. Added bonuses of a university include extended hours for tutoring, excellent libraries, larger selection of courses, sports teams, and student centers that may include exercise rooms and swimming pools. Also, the availability of grants, loans, and scholarships is much higher. On the negative side, you may feel lost in the crowd at a huge university.

Ask the same questions for these schools as you did for community college, and also consider you may want to attend graduate school.

Private College

You may be interested in attending a private college for a variety of reasons. Private colleges may be perfectly credible, but always check to confirm the school you choose is accredited.[1] Also, you need to ensure your credits will be accepted elsewhere in case you choose to transfer. Two nice things about a private college are smaller class sizes and specific programs and activities, such as a Christian education for those seeking such. If you're a religious person, this option may be appealing because of the opportunity to take a Bible class or attending religious services. This keeps many people accountable. However, private colleges are usually more expensive, so this option might not be the most viable for you. Be sure to investigate their fees so you can decide if you're willing to take out loans or pay extra money out of pocket.

Technical or Vocational School

If you have a specific field in mind that requires a license, a technical school might be your best option. These schools focus on cosmetology, administrative work, engineering, massage, acupuncture, mechanics, and agriculture—to name a few. Many vocational schools focus on medical assisting and licensed vocational nursing (a step below registered nurse). These colleges can move you through the certification process quickly, but may also cost a lot of money when they're profit-seeking businesses owned by private companies. Often these schools offer less financial aid, so be sure to thoroughly research

---

1   See the Resources section for a link to accreditation database.

this option. And as a note, you can earn many technical and vocational certificates at a community college or university.

Online Education

Are you hoping to work from home as a student? Nearly all community colleges, universities, and private schools offer online classes or entirely online programs. Some schools are completely online. This is a great option because you can be home and save money on child care. For all these options, the online courses will either be synchronous (live meeting times online) or asynchronous (delayed, work on your own, but report by a certain day). This is an important question to ask when speaking to an admissions or academic counselor since you may need one or the other, depending on your schedule. Once again, be careful when selecting an online college, as many are for-profit and some aren't even accredited — which means their units won't transfer or their degrees aren't held to the same standard as others.

Only you can make the decision about where you want to attend college. Painstaking research is your best tool. Visit each school you're interested in, getting a feel for the campus and students. Make an appointment with an advisor. Look at their degree programs and be sure they offer exactly what you're looking for. Also look at reviews from other students or alumni who were willing to give honest opinions about each college. If you can meet a mom who successfully completed college there, even better! Always be sure to check for accreditation and review the financial aid. In my experience, you shouldn't have to pay out of pocket unless you have left-over fees after financial aid. Be smart and cautious with whatever choices you make.

Chapter 3

Balancing School and Family

I'ESHA

"*I encourage any mom to go back to school, no matter what the age of your child. You will set an example of hard work and the value of education. Do not let fear, doubt, or finances be the determining factor. I feared my ability to handle the responsibilities of being a student and the duties of being a mom, but having my daughter motivated me to keep going and secure our financial future.*"

"HOW DO YOU find the time?" That's the most common question people ask when they learn I'm attending college. The truth is, during every semester I fall behind and feel overwhelmed by the demands of school and family life. I cringe inside when a professor assigns extra reading material or one of my children joins a sports team. Yet, I always make it to the finish line (final exams) and do well.

How? By managing time in a way that keeps me going forward even when I want to hide in the bedroom closet. When the procrastination monster comes calling I try to defeat it before things get out of hand. I follow a consistent study routine based on rules I set for myself. And, I find creative ways to spend time with my kids without breaking our fragile bank account.

Time Management

Managing time is one of the biggest struggles for college students—parents or not. It seems we have so much time, and then before we know it, midterm arrives and we haven't read the last three chapters of the textbook. Yes, catching up is possible, but I find it much easier to avoid falling behind. Here are some tips for effectively managing your time:

1. **Write everything down.** Find a planner that works for your lifestyle. I prefer using both a paper planner and the calendar on my phone as a backup. My favorite is a daily planner and my newest, the Passion Planner. This book is hour-by-hour as opposed to morning, noon, and evening, and also has room for assignments near the bottom of the page. It may seem a bit crazy, but avoiding procrastination is easier when you map out your entire day. Don't just write down your class times. Instead, include appointments, time for travelling to and from school, study sessions, and time for your family. Once you start doing this, it will be easy to stick to a plan. . .but don't forget to add time for yourself, however short it may be

2. **Don't be a hero.** As a mom, you *are* a hero, but that doesn't mean you're superhuman. As a human like the rest of us, only take a course load you think you can handle. If your academic schedule will severely limit study time and family time, it's too much. Yes, we want to finish school, but it isn't worth it to sacrifice all our time in order to get it done.

3. **Designate a Homework Free day.** Give yourself and your family a break! I used to study every single day, always falling asleep at the end of the day with some type of homework in my hand. I didn't know how to say no and put the homework away. I was, and still am, worried I'll be forever behind if I take a day off. However, I learned that having one day off from homework can help in the end. Make it a priority to have a day with no homework where you focus on your family, your home, and yourself. You won't regret it!

4. **Prioritize your tasks.** Whether it's home, school, kids, or work, do your best to set priorities. Now, don't get me wrong, children are a top priority, but in day-to-day life you also have other things to do. Every day get up and write a priority list. If something is due at noon, don't wait until 11:30 to start. If your child has an appointment, commit to it. While life will always throw in sudden changes, you'll feel calmer if you have a prioritized schedule.

5. **Practice good study habits.** This will be a section in itself, but to sum it up: don't cram, study in an environment conducive to learning, pay attention in class, and ask for help as needed. For more on this topic, keep reading.

6. **Consider timing.** Before registering for classes, consider your schedule, your spouse's schedule, (if applicable), and your children. Is your college close enough for you to attend classes while the kids are in school? If so, you

may be able to work day classes into your schedule. A large number of moms work during the day and choose to attend classes in the evening. You have to find the schedule that works best for your situation.

7. **Keep your eyes on the prize.** You're going to college for a reason, and keeping your goals in mind will help you stay on track. As moms we already wear a lot of hats, but I truly believe that revisiting your goals will help you stay motivated and keep your forward momentum. It's easy to fall behind and feel discouraged when life throws us a variety of curveballs on a daily and weekly basis. Regardless of what may come your way, your motivation to complete college can be enough to carry you forward.

Effective Studying

The rule of thumb states that each week you should study for two hours outside class for every unit (credit) you're enrolled. If you're taking a three-unit course, you can expect to study six hours outside class. Adding up a full-time semester (12 units), that's 24 hours of studying. I don't know about you, but just the thought of finding 24 hours a week makes me anxious. That's why effective studying is important. Yes, you've studied most of your life, but are you truly getting the most out of each study session? Have you ever found yourself staring at a page for over twenty minutes without reading a single word? Do you send texts and check emails while you're supposed to be studying? Do you frequently panic because you waited until the last minute? These habits are totally ineffective. Over time I found study routines that use my time and energy in the most effective way:

1. **Turn off your phone.** This is a huge elephant in the room, so we'll get it out of the way first. Yes, I know we need to be connected in case something happens with our kids, but that doesn't mean we need to be constantly

interrupted. Shut down your phone or place it in the next room. If you can't bear to part with it, at least turn off notifications for all those fun things we like to enjoy while distracting ourselves from responsibility. Another way to avoid interference from your phone is to set a special ringtone for your babysitter or home phone number. That way, you won't miss an emergency call.

2. **Don't cram.** I cannot emphasize this enough — cramming is not effective learning. Don't wait until the last minute to study, because you're likely to forget everything you crammed into your brain at the last minute. I used to be that person sitting in the classroom before a final exam, doing my best to somehow learn one more fact before the professor told us to put our notes away. Right after I put my notes away, everything I thought I'd captured flew right out the window. Eventually I learned that from the moment I walk into the classroom, whatever I know at that point is what I have to work with. Cramming won't help you ace an exam and it certainly won't allow you to retain information for a long time.

3. **Read your textbooks.** And read them like a student! How so? First, use questions at the end of each chapter as a guideline while reading. Even though it's always good to close-read a text, reading the questions first will help you recognize what's most important — and steer you in the direction that best prepares you for upcoming homework and exams. Second, have a conversation with the text. By that, I mean you need to respond to certain remarks, questions, or statements. Use the margin of your text (or a piece of paper if you don't plan on keeping the textbook) to ask questions and record your thoughts. Reading a textbook is not like reading a novel for pleasure. You have to keep a keen eye out for clear (and sometimes unclear) points. Also,

take notes as you read and highlight things covered by the professor in class. These items will probably show up on exams.

4. **Get your rest!** Whenever possible, get enough sleep at night. While we mothers tend to operate on pure exhaustion, being a student changes things a bit. There's no point in staying up late to study when you probably won't retain that information. Instead, give your noggin a break and start fresh the next day. As mothers we already lack the adequate amount of suggested sleep on a nightly basis; we should not cut that time in half because of homework.

5. **Focus on one subject at a time.** It's important to work on one assignment at a time, but not for a long period of time. I suggest studying in 30-minute intervals, taking a 5 to 10-minute break, and then either returning to the same assignment or switching to another. If you feel stuck on a particular topic, move on and come back later. You aren't being productive when you're questioning the material in front of you in an unproductive way. Additionally, you should prioritize assignments by asking yourself certain questions, such as: "When is this due?" or "How much of my grade depends on this particular assignment?" Of course all assignments are important, but if you spend all your time working on an assignment worth 5% while your 20% paper gathers dust, things will not end well.

6. **Be an active learner.** This is simple: Show up to class, complete your homework, participate, ask questions, take notes, and pay attention. You invested time and money in your college education, so do your best to be completely present during class time. When I first started school I continually worried about something happening to my kids while I was unavailable. I would mentally check out and obsess over worst-case scenarios.

However, nothing major ever happened and, in the end, my biggest regret was not paying attention. Shyness and insecurity can also keep you from being an active learner, especially as a mom in college. I struggled with insecurity for most of my undergraduate education and never sought advice. From me to you, I'm going to tell you the truth: Some classmates may find you weird, while others may choose you as a study partner first because they know you'll get your work done. Other students may be intimidated by you. I learned my insecurity was self-inflicted almost all the time. I want you to remember that when you enter a classroom filled with freshman and sophomores during your first day at a transfer school (or any other time). You are not alone. You are unique—and awesome! Be an active member of every class, and you may soon become a leader who sets an example for younger students.

7. **Find a dedicated study group.** You've probably experienced the opposite of a dedicated study group. I know this because I've been in "that" study group where no one actually studies and instead we laugh and have fun. From a seasoned study grouper, these are pointers on finding awesome study group members:

   a. Don't study with your best friend. It's just not a great idea to study with someone with whom you can chat about anything for hours. During these study sessions, I accomplished next to nothing. Instead, find people you don't know well in your class or in your major.

   b. Someone you know who is driven and motivated. Especially if you're still learning to be a better student, this person's work ethic and determination will influence you.

   c. Students you've met in the re-entry, parenting, or childcare center are great study partners. If you need to bring your children and study elsewhere (like a park or at home), that would probably discourage students who don't have children. Studying with other parents allows you all to bring your kids or gives you a group of people who don't mind having children around.

d. For numbers, I recommend no more than six people. Having a large group can create problems with noise and other interruptions. It may also limit your ability to snag a smaller study room on campus.

8. **Give yourself a break.** My mentor always told our class, "An hour a day, then go out and play." I do my best to follow this advice all the time. Yes, sometimes we have to study more within a day's time, but we shouldn't sit in a study area for 12 hours a day. You can't learn like that. Instead, spend a few hours every day and then stop. You deserve a break.

Family Time

As moms and college students we wear many hats. One thing I know is that you and I need to take off a few hats now and then, and not keep adding extra hats. How do we manage to keep the "awesome student" hat balanced on our heads while also wearing the "awesome mom" and possibly the "awesome wife/girlfriend" hat? Seems impossible, but I've come to realize there are ways to do this. However, before I get to these tips, I want to suggest doing one thing before you begin school:

Talk about this new stage in your life with your entire family. Your children (and partner/spouse) may be used to having you home a lot, but that will temporarily change. Talk about the time requirements, the days you'll be gone, and when you plan to study. Also bring up the importance of pursuing and finishing your degree. Please be sure to involve your family in this experience because they are impacted by your choices and will be there to cheer you on at graduation.

1. **Don't over schedule.** Don't add things to your schedule when you know you can't handle any more on your plate. I know you want to do as much as possible, and if you have free time you think the world is nearly ending; I promise you it is not ending. You need to leave open time for your family outside of dinner and homework time. Even a short break is important. One way to prevent overscheduling is to use a planner. For a sample schedule please visit the resources page at the end of this book.

2. **Turn off your phone, laptop, tablet, or any other device that keeps you tethered.** Yes, I already said this, but I can't stress how important it to disconnect and spend quality time with your family. I turn off my phone for a while every day. I also do my best to disconnect myself from social media. Why? Because it's overwhelming! Do I like some aspects of social media? You bet I do! On the other hand, people begin expecting you to post and be constantly present. The point is, this becomes another hat we wear—the social media butterfly. Stop. Just stop. Step away from that part of life and enjoy the silence. Enjoy your children and your significant other. Take delight in things you enjoy in the simplest moments—the moments that don't require logging in and posting your status.

3. **Let someone help where help is needed.** If you're struggling in school with a certain class and your friend offers to help, for crying out loud accept the offer. If one of your mom-friends or a relative offer to babysit so you can study or get away with your significant other: take them up on that offer. You may not be able to remove all your hats for a long time, but please allow yourself time to go hat-less now and then.

4. **The toughest thing: Say NO.** If you're like me, you don't like saying no to anyone or anything. But sometimes you have to. You aren't responsible for everyone in the world or all the things they expect and want from you. You answer to only yourself and whomever you choose to answer to, and you don't owe people an explanation about why you're saying no. Anyone who tries to get an explanation out of you clearly doesn't understand how busy you are as a mom and student, among other roles you take on. Say no. Just say it.

5. **Don't feel pressured to go over the top.** Spending time with your kids doesn't have to be a grand production. Your children just want *you*: It's that simple. But what can you do with them? While you're in college and not able to manage all the fun stuff other parents might be doing with their kids, here's my list of fun, free, or low cost activities:

    a. **Build a fort.** Come on; don't even try to tell me you don't still dream about building an epic fort out of blankets and then disappearing into another world! This activity is free and fun. It allows you to spend time with your kids while they practice pretend-play. Not skilled in the blanket-fort-making industry? Do a DIY Internet search and be impressed!

    b. **Have a movie night.** If you have the finances to go to a theater and watch a new movie, more power to ya! However, if you don't, then make your den or living room the theater. Grab popcorn and bowls, pick out a movie (or two) everyone will enjoy, close the curtains, and cuddle up on the couch. This is a family favorite in our house and we try to do it every Friday. Also do your best to schedule a movie night with your spouse or partner. My husband and I try to either go out to the movies or pick something from home. Either way, we always end up spending time alone, which is rare but wonderful.

c. **Go to the park.** Kids need fresh air and so do you! Allow your children to explore the playground for a while, and then create a learning experience by having them look for certain things like bugs, flowers, or types of trees. If you want to take it a step further, bring disposable gloves and trash bags and, as a family, collect litter. It's best to have the kids point out the litter and hold the bag while you pick up the trash and throw it in. Not your cup of tea? Invest in a soccer ball.

d. **Cook together.** I know it can be madness to have kids under your feet while you attempt to make dinner, so instead of trying to get them out of the kitchen, include them. One child can be in charge of measuring ingredients, one can be in charge of stirring, and so on. Once again, you are encouraging teamwork among your children, which is great. This is also another great way to bond with your partner or spouse.

e. **Write a book together, or read.** You don't have to write a novel or anything, just a book or a few books. You can create the book with simple paper. Include illustrations drawn with crayons or markers to make it just like a picture book. This activity is not only cheap (or free if you have the items), but also encourages creativity and promotes writing practice and literacy. This can become an ongoing series-based story that can span many weeks of writing and reading. Additionally, reading is crucial for your children and you. If you have school-aged children, they should be reading at least 30 minutes a day after school. What better way to spend quality time than opening a book and escaping to another world together?

f. **Do homework together.** If you absolutely can't skip out on studying, do it together. Some of my best study times were with my children. I know this isn't always a perfect experience, but it's worth trying. Not only will you all get your work done, you are also inspiring and encouraging your children to study and do their best. If your partner or spouse is also attending college, schedule your study times together.

g. **Visit museums and other places of interest.** This option can be for fun and education, or to complete a classroom assignment. As long as children are permitted, it's is a great way to spend time together while also getting your work done. I've done this on a few occasions, including the time I had to visit a botanical garden and chose to bring my eldest son along. He was about eight years old at the time, so I had him bring along a "field journal" just as I was required to do, and him to write about what he saw. We had an absolute blast. There's nothing better than learning together.

h. **Commit to a date night with your partner/ spouse.** My husband and I have struggled with this commitment, usually because of money issues or the fact that we have four children and worry they'll overrun the house while being cared for by someone else. However, we do our best to at least have a lunch date every other week. I recommend that, either once a week or every other week, you commit to leaving the house with your partner/ spouse and enjoy time together. While it may be just a few short hours, this gives you time to enjoy each other's company outside of the house. Please do not sacrifice this time.

I realize none of this is rocket science—and I don't intend it to be. I think it helps to have another mom tell you these things. I know it helps me. Being a mom is a tough job, and being a mom in college can become overwhelming to the point that you give up. Instead of reaching the breaking point where you feel overwhelmed by the weight of a dozen hats on your head, why not take off a hat or two? You deserve to rest your head, your heart, and your body just like everyone else. Now go ahead. Come on. Remove a few of those hats!

Chapter 4

Find Support on Campus

Liz

> *"Campus organizations and clubs were a surprising source of support for me. While our college is small, they offer an amazing variety of clubs and activities. I am grateful for the incredible support and encouragement I receive from the staff, administration, and faculty at my college."*

DO YOU KNOW if your campus has a childcare center? What about a re-entry center? When I first started community college I was unaware of the support services available to students. I spent many semesters with unnecessary worry that caused extra stress on top of my responsibilities as a student and mother. Eventually I took the time to explore campus, only to discover my school had several programs for moms like me. In this chapter I will introduce a few important centers to look for on campus. Even though I made it through my community college experience without several of these, I wish I'd found them in time.

Financial Aid

As moms, we are usually strapped for cash. Even if we save money and live frugal lives, we have more expenses than the average student, and the children's needs come first. Besides tuition, you'll need to pay for books and transportation. One of the first things you should do when considering college is visit the financial aid office on campus. They will probably help you fill out a FAFSA (Free Application for Student Aid) online. The form can be a bit tedious, but it opens doors and windows to various forms of financial assistance including loans, grants, and scholarships.

The financial aid office is also a great place to visit if you have questions about scholarships and on-campus programs for low-income students. Don't be too proud to explore these resources—even if you think you make too much money to qualify. Having money for textbooks (which can be incredibly expensive, especially in certain majors), tuition, supplies, and other expenses takes a lot of stress off your shoulders. Along with the financial aid office, keep your eyes peeled for scholarship opportunities at many of the centers I'm about to introduce to you.

Academic Counseling/Advising

Beginning can be stressful when you don't know where to begin or what's expected of you. I felt lost the first day I walked onto campus. Thankfully, someone pointed to the academic counseling center, where I learned about orientation, assessments, and registering for class. I met with a counselor who discussed resources and how long it would to complete my degree and/or transfer. She offered personal tips and tricks on registering for classes and what classes to take as a returning student. This experience allowed me to begin with more positive outlook, which was especially important for me because of past difficulties with school. Here are some of the great services counseling centers provide:

1. **Academic Counseling.** At the counseling center, you'll either meet with someone right away or make an appointment to return. Your new counselor will ask about your plans, goals, and educational background in order to help you make an academic plan. This plan

will cover your next two to four semesters, including all required classes and the electives you choose. During the meeting you should talk about your worries regarding college and mention the areas where you might need extra help. For example, if your math, writing, or reading skills are weak, the counselor might recommend special classes or workshops to build your competency (and your confidence) before you take required subjects. The counselor will also know which classes are rigorous and time consuming. She should encourage you to spread these out over two or three semesters.

2. **Success Workshops.** Some counseling centers offer special workshops on topics such studying, note taking, mindfulness, and time management. College is much different than high school, especially for a mom. Getting through college requires abilities that may be rusty if you've been away from school for a while. You'll need patience, planning, and study skills. The counseling center can help reduce stress and allow you to have a great college experience.

3. **Help when you need to take a break.** As a mom in college you may need to take a leave of absence for various reasons. The counseling center can support your decision to leave, make sure you leave nothing up in the air before you go, and help plan your reentry.

4. **Connections.** If the counseling center doesn't have something you need, they can find it for you. From career training to the location of the testing or tutoring center – they can help. Most of the counselors connect with other departments in order to advocate for students and make sure their experience is smooth and successful. Ask your counselor to point you in the right direction for whatever you may need.

Tutoring/Writing Center/Library

Whether you're new to college or already a student, three of the best academic resources on every campus are the:

learning and tutoring center,

the writing center,

and the library.

You might be out of practice or struggling with classes like math and English, the two subjects most commonly supported by the learning and writing centers. At the tutoring center you can receive help free of charge—you don't have to fall behind because you don't understand something. You'll probably meet with a tutor for one-on-one assistance for thirty-minutes at a time. The library is an excellent center for help with research as well as being a quiet place to study and do homework. The librarians can help you find scholarly articles you might need for English, history, or other writing-intensive courses. They can request materials for you if your library doesn't have them. Don't hesitate to get help from these centers; they might make the difference between an A and a B.

Mental Health Counseling

I've gone quite a few semesters feeling as though I didn't have anyone to talk with about certain issues. I love my family and friends, but they tend to give positive feedback and offer me solutions. Sometimes I don't want answers to my problems; I need an ear to listen. Doing well in college was a triumph for me, but the stress took a toll on my mental health. I know this may be true for you as well.

If you feel overwhelmed and don't have someone to talk with, please consider visiting your campus mental health counseling center. While academic counseling will help you master the academic rigors of school, a mental health counselor can help with emotional struggles, anxiety, and possible learning difficulties. This is a place where you can talk about how you really feel. Your sessions are confidential and the counselor isn't permitted to share your conversations with others unless your life is in immediate danger. If you need help, do not hesitate to make an appointment or drop by—they are there for you.

Women's Center

What better place to seek help than a center devoted to women? If you find a women's center on your campus, please visit often. The Women's Center on my campus is my favorite place for several reasons. First, I love this center because they advocate for all genders, not just women. They are seriously involved in such issues as being a parent, domestic violence prevention and intervention, and time/stress management. They want to make sure students are protected, both in and outside the classroom. They provide resources, pamphlets, advice, and advocacy. You may also connect with other moms at this center. I made a few friends there, and it's nice to see each other and talk about our busy lives once in a while. The Women's Center is a must-visit place on campus.

Re-Entry Center

Many of you are re-entry or nontraditional students, or both. Re-entry means you're returning to school after an extended period of time. Members of this group are over twenty-five and often have children and work full time. The Re-entry Center can help you research previous classes to see if your credits still apply. This is especially true for students who return after a decade or more. Like the Women's Center, the Re-entry Center provides workshops and helps us connect with peers. They also foster student-parent clubs and scholarships aimed directly at students like us. Check it out!

Disabled Student Services Center

This center is important if you're disabled in any way. At the DSS center you'll find resources for a variety of issues. If you have a learning disability, visit this office to receive the learning assistance you need. Even if you suspect you have a learning disability but have never been tested, your college may offer a free assessment program. The same goes for those with physical and health-related disabilities. The Disabled Student Services Center will advocate for you. This even includes pregnant women, especially those considered high risk. If you need help, don't hesitate to visit this office and start the process.

Health Center

Access to health care isn't cheap or easy, and getting in to see a doctor might be difficult with your busy schedule. One benefit of being a full time college student is receiving free healthcare on many campuses. If you're sick, injured, or need vaccinations, these things may be available to you. If the clinic staff can't help with something, they'll refer you to a provider in your community. This may not seem like something you need at the moment, but when mid-semester exhaustion hits, the cold or flu may not be too far behind. Use the resources your school provides.

Childcare Center

Of all the resources that help me as a mom in college, the Children's Center at Cal State Fullerton ranks number one. Leaving my kids at home hurts my heart every time. And while I couldn't take my older kids who are in school, my youngest son went to college with me for two years. That is one of the coolest experiences I've had as a mom. I know many of you feel uncomfortable about leaving your children with someone you don't know well. I understand that. But what better people to work with your kids than employees of a center that constantly trains and monitors their staff? Here's why I recommend signing up your little ones for your college's childcare center:

1. **It's on campus.** Leaving your child behind is hard, so wouldn't it help to have them nearby? I loved knowing my son was just a short walk away from me, having fun and learning new things. I also loved knowing the employees could easily find me in case of an emergency. Having my son on campus alleviated so much stress. Also, picking him up was a breeze.

2. **Low cost or no cost.** If not free, then cheap! Childcare is difficult to afford for anyone, especially single moms. If you are low-income, you might qualify for free (subsidized) care. This can be a huge relief when you're struggling to make ends meet.

3. **Highly trained staff.** While all childcare centers have trained and certificated staff, staff members at the college childcare centers are usually enrolled in child development classes, or they completed that training and are teaching others. Standards are high, following the latest and most helpful techniques for helping young learners, both academically and behaviorally. My husband and I were skeptical at first, but we soon trusted our campus' childcare center one hundred percent.

4. **Study time.** One of the great benefits of the childcare center is they often allow you time to study. This varies from school to school, but in order to help you be more successful you can include study time into your requested hours of care. For example, at my university I was allowed two hours of study time per week for every unit I enrolled in. That is a LOT of study time. I didn't use all that time, but it came in handy when I needed to stay on campus and get stuff done.

5. **Connect with other parents.** At the childcare center I absolutely loved talking to other moms and dads, and even became friends with a few professors. Dealing with the center will open your eyes to different types of people on campus, including school employees, professors, undergraduates, and graduate students. We all have the same goal as parents: to give our kids the best. Who knows, you might meet a new study friend, a babysitter, someone who'd like to start a play group, or a future professor.

Student Housing

While this subtopic might not apply to you, I want to briefly include housing, because it's a resource many nontraditional students don't know about. While being in a traditional dorm isn't possible, some colleges and universities offer family housing. Located on or near campus, these facilities usually accommodate a small family with two to three bedrooms. This type of family housing is often much cheaper than normal rental prices in the area. Visit the housing department on your campus to learn more about housing opportunities.

I wish I could name all the services available to you as a mom in college, but each school is different. Please explore your campus and your school's web page, because you may find unexpected help and support. Being a mom in college can be stressful, especially when you see other students enjoying themselves while you rush back home to children and a job. You may feel there's nothing for you on campus, but trust me, there is. You just need to look for it. Finding help through these various centers and resources is one way to take control of your education and make it better.

Chapter 5

Funding Your Education

CHARLENE

"My divorce had been filed and my ex-husband stopped helping with the bills. I felt like I was drowning. I thought long and hard about my next step: Should I go back to retail and make the money we desperately needed, or continue to better myself for the future? I chose to stay and continue with college, determined to see this through."

IN A PERFECT world I wouldn't have to write this chapter; but I can't write a college success guide without including advice on funding your education. Some people drop out of college because they can't afford to take time away from work, can't find a job that works around their class schedule, and either don't qualify for financial aid or don't understand the available options. You may be struggling with one or all of these issues.

During my time in college I learned important lessons about how to fund an education from grants, loans, and scholarships. When I first started college I already knew about some options. As I continued in school, I learned about the benefits of other avenues such as campus jobs, scholarships, and loans. And while I don't recommend taking out loans as a first choice, I urge you to educate yourself on the options. This chapter will explain both the process and the choices.

Fill Out the FAFSA

If you've never attended college, you may be puzzled by the anagram, FAFSA. This is the online form known as the Free Application for Federal Student Aid,[2] and it's the key to many financial assistance options. This annual form is a must-do on your college checklist. The process can be daunting the first few times you fill it out, so here are my quick tips:

1. Visit https://fafsa.ed.gov on a secure browser. You will be entering sensitive information and the last thing you need is a stolen identity.

2. Before you log in, be sure to have everything you need: If you're completing the form after filing your taxes (most people complete the form around the end of February), then have your tax forms ready (1040, 540, etc.). If you haven't filed yet, use your last paycheck of the previous year, which allows you to select the "haven't filed yet" option and return later to update with your tax information.

3. Sign up, create your login and then record that information in a spot where you won't lose it. I won't lie: I've forgotten my login more times than I care to admit.

4. Enter your personal information. Please be accurate and double check everything. You don't want the process slowed because you entered a nickname instead of your legal name.

5. Enter financial information. This is where those tax forms come in. Once again, accuracy is the key.

6. Search for your school or schools. Yes, you may enter multiple colleges if you're applying to more than one school, OR if you plan to take classes at more than one. Be sure you add them all to the selection list.

7. Sign the form with your new ID number/name, and submit.

2   https://fafsa.ed.gov

8. Wait. You should an e-mail saying your form was successfully accepted. Some time before registration at your chosen college, you will receive an award letter. Don't stress over the Expected Family Contribution (EFC) just yet. If that number is zero, you will definitely receive financial aid. However, you can still receive some aid if it isn't zero.

Grants

Now that you've filled out the form, lets discuss your first line of financial assistance—the grant. This assistance comes in several forms and is money you don't have to pay back, by the way. The most well-known option is the Federal Pell Grant, with the maximum annual allotment at approximately $6,000. This grant does have a time/allowance limit, so be sure to track your usage and award amounts. Check the website to find the current time/allowance limit, as it will likely change.

The same goes for any state grants you may be awarded. In California this money is aptly named the Cal Grant. Check with your financial aid office to get connected to the state website where you can gather information on this grant. It's likely your financial aid office will award it to you without anything beyond the FAFSA.

Finally, many universities offer grants of their own, and I've noticed these are usually awarded to students who don't qualify for the other two options. So, if you're working full-time, there's still hope for you if your annual income is above the cut-off for the previous two grants. Once again, this will probably be awarded without your intervention.

Grants are the best option when it comes to funding, because they're awarded based on financial need alone. And, as I mentioned above, you don't have to pay them back unless you drop out of a semester after spending the money. If that happens, please visit your financial aid office immediately.

Waivers

This section may or may not apply to you. If you're attending a California community college, it most definitely does. If not, I suggest checking with your desired college or university to see if they have something similar. California offers a Board of Governors Fee Waiver—a wonderful benefit for community college students who qualify for financial aid. If you qualify, your unit fees are waived. As with the Pell Grant, this waiver has a time/unit limit, so be sure to check into this.

Loans

I approach this section with caution, and I'd like you to do the same. When I first started college I had no idea I could apply for a loan from the government and I'm so glad I didn't know. Otherwise, I would now be burdened with loan payments for student debt. However, as a transfer student I did have to take out loans for the last two years of my undergraduate education and for graduate school. There's nothing wrong with accepting these loans, but you need to get all the facts, because student loan debt can ruin your life.

What are your options? Through the government, you can receive loans known as the William D. Ford Federal Direct Loan (Direct Loan) Program.[3] This includes several types of loans, including the most common:

1. Subsidized Loan. This type of loan does not accrue interest while you're attending college. This is the *friendly loan*, as I like to call it. Loan amounts vary and that information can be found at https://studentaid. ed.gov. Once again, this loan will may offered to you, but from my experience, only at the four-year college level. However, the loan is also available to community college students, so do consult with your school's financial aid office.

---

3   https://studentaid.ed.gov/sa/types/loans#types

2. Unsubsidized Loan. I like to call this the *somewhat friendly loan* that starts tracking your debt right away. This loan is less-desirable because interest immediately begins accruing. I recommend taking this loan ONLY if you're in a dire situation and truly need it—and if you have a reasonable plan to pay back the money.

3. Private Loans. Some banks and employers offer private loans for education. Consult with your bank and/or employer to find out options.

4. Federal Perkins Loan. This one is for students in need of financial assistance beyond the normal award allotment. These loans come directly from the schools.

A few extra thoughts on loans: You will receive loan counselling before you can access the funds, so if any of this confuses you, the counselling will help clarify such terms as *interest* and *deferral*. Loan counselling is an online process, but I recommend attending an information session on loans if your college offers one. Most importantly, if you take out loans, begin paying them back as soon as possible. I started paying back my loans right away, in order to decrease the interest so my total at the end of graduate school isn't as high as it could be.

After finishing college you'll have a six-month deferral period when no payments are due. However, as long as you're in school you don't have to pay. Additionally, there are repayment plans depending on your income level, so don't hesitate to contact your loan servicer to find out the best option for your situation. But please remember, loans should be your last resort for financial assistance in college.

Here's what happened to someone I know: Roy, a 35-year old single father with two sons, wanted to better himself by attending college. He had a good job with UPS, but wanted to be a college graduate and have a professional career. Roy worked hard to earn a 4-year degree in psychology and the college counselors told him he'd have no problem finding a job. The reality? Six years later, Roy is still working for UPS. After graduating he discovered that entry level jobs in psychology do not pay well enough for him to support his kids *and* make the loan payments. The longer he waits, the harder it is for him to find a job in his field. In other words, the very loans that allowed Roy to graduate from college are now keeping him from the job he wants.

Many college graduates who face this same Catch-22 situation end up living with their parents. Some of these graduates discover entry level salaries aren't adequate, so they apply for graduate school in order to defer the loan payments and earn a better salary after graduation. But eventually they have to begin paying the original loans, plus the extra loans. Think long and hard about this. As you consider student loans, look ahead several years to your future budget and consider these questions:

- How much money do you and your family need every month?
- What will your monthly loan payments be?
- How likely is it you'll find a great job before these payments begin?
- How much would you make per month at an entry level job in your new profession?

Now, see how your budget looks. Can you handle those payments? In Chapter Six we'll take a closer look at choosing a profession that will allow you to enjoy your work and still support your family.

Another consideration: Before you decide on a school, visit the campus career office and investigate their record for helping graduates find employment. Don't accept everything they tell you. Go online and look at jobs and salaries in your major. You don't want to graduate with a degree you won't be able to use. (You'll read more about this in Chapter Six).

Scholarships

Before I transferred to Cal State Fullerton I had not won scholarships from my community college. On my campus, being a college mom was fairly common, which made the applicant pool for scholarships competitive. Plus, I didn't understand how to apply for off-campus scholarships. After I transferred to a four-year university I won scholarships every semester as an undergraduate and graduate student. I was blown away after the first award letter and continued to feel grateful every time. Because I know the importance of scholarships for students like us, I want to tell you more about your options and give you tips on finding, applying, and winning cash for your education.

On-Campus Scholarships

The first way to can find scholarships is through your college campus. This is my most successful approach, and I've won every scholarship by applying through the university's online scholarship application forms. The scholarships I've won include a parent-student scholarship from the Associated Student Body, a nontraditional scholarship from the Re-entry Center, and a graduate student endowment. Overall, I won over $6,000 in scholarships simply by taking the time to fill out the application.

How can you do this?

Find out how your college conducts the application process, and then search for specific scholarships through your major department. Some require a separate application. Regardless, fill out the general college application so any possible matches can be offered. Once you begin filling out the application, be sure you secure a letter of recommendation from a professor who knows you well. If you've only been in college a short time, choose the professor you had the best experience with. Please give the professor ample time to write the letter—at least two weeks, but a month is even better. Next, include a personal statement. Some applications ask for specific details in the statement. If you need help with this, visit the writing center on campus or your favorite English professor. This letter needs to describe your struggles (without whining) and also point out your financial need. Further, you need to talk about the future. This can be tricky if you aren't sure what the future holds. Please see the resource pages at the back of this book for an example of a personal statement.

On campus, you're most likely to win scholarships based on your demographic. While quite a few moms attend college nowadays, the number of moms who apply is still smaller than the overall number of applicants. Donors want their money to go to the most qualified and deserving candidate—and with so much on your plate while still maintaining your grades, that candidate might be you!

Off-Campus Scholarships

Winning off-campus scholarships can be an amazing experience, because you're competing with a larger applicant pool. If you win, you've really impressed someone. However, I want to pause for a moment to tell you this: If you don't win, that is not a marker of some personal deficiency. It's not your fault. Instead, remember that, depending on the scholarship, only a certain number of people can be chosen and someone who either had a stronger application or more financial need, won. You did your best and you are still amazing! Keep trying, that's the best advice I can give you.

But where should you look? When it comes to winning scholarships off-campus, there are many options: banks (especially credit unions), honor societies, websites, organizations, etc. One of the most popular websites to search for scholarships is FastWeb.com. Once you sign up and enter your basic and educational information, the website gives you a list of possible matches. My only tip is to use caution and read all requirements and rules.

Honor societies are another off-campus resource for scholarships. Are you a member of a society such as Phi Theta Kappa or Phi Kappa Phi? Do you belong to a major-specific society? All these groups offer scholarships, so be sure to visit the website of any society you belong to. Oh, and if you aren't currently affiliated with a group, head over to Chapter 8 and find out why you should be! Last, some churches offer scholarships. If you belong to a particular religion, you may be eligible.

Keep in mind that scholarships are offered on and off campus throughout the year, with due dates once a year in either the fall or spring semester/quarter (and sometimes, summer), so be sure to research each scholarship you find. For each scholarship you investigate, note the due date, required GPA, demographic requirements, and academic level (junior, senior, etc.). Once you know the due dates, grab your planner and mark the due date with a reminder six weeks before that day, giving you ample time to write and gather the required essays or letters of recommendation.

No matter where you search for scholarships, the one fact that remains true is that you can't win if you don't apply. As a mom in college, you'll find many scholarships you're eligible for. Trust me, it's worth the effort!

Campus Employment

Depending on your employment status and availability, working on campus may be another way to earn money and gain valuable experience. I worked as a student-employee several times on both my community college and university campuses. I loved these jobs! The environment is fast-paced and you get to see your college campus from a new perspective. Furthermore, campus jobs are required to work with your class schedule and can only allow you to work 20 hours a week (in most places, but check with your college). Therefore, you won't feel overwhelmed between work, school, and kids. When it comes to landing a job on campus, you'll find three options: federal work study, student assistant, or staff member.

Federal work study is a position on campus paid through federal funding, usually related to community service and/or your major. This allows both undergraduate and graduate students to work for additional funding while earning a degree. As a student with either full or part-time enrollment, you're awarded a work-study allowance and then earn an hourly wage, paid at least once a month. I think this form of financial aid is great for those who feel bad about receiving help from the government. You have to work for the money, which justifies receiving the funds. Furthermore, the jobs are not long term, so you don't feel obligated to remain in a specific position after the designated award period. Be sure to check with the financial aid office and your career center to get more details.

If you don't qualify for work study or would rather not choose that option, you can apply to be a **student assistant** on campus. These positions include office assistants, lab assistants, interpreters, note-takers, tutors, cashiers, and more. I happened to work in the humanities division office at my community college where the bulk of my work was administrative duties. I loved this job. I met students, connected with professors, and made lasting friendships and network connections. Working on campus gives you up close and personal experience with people you hope to emulate one day in your own career. While you work with them, you're also learning. These jobs are either broadcast on the campus portal or directly on the campus career website.

Another way to make money on campus is to gain employment as an actual **staff member**. While I can't speak for all campuses, I do know you can't be both a student and a staff employee concurrently, so be sure to check on such restrictions. Working as a campus staff member opens many doors concerning pay, experience, benefits, and quite possibly, tuition reimbursement or waivers. The benefit of free tuition for college employees is a wonderful thing. Having your tuition waived would save a lot of money, so research your college's employee benefits.

Funding your education is one of the most crucial parts of college because it saves you money and allows you to keep attending school. You're more likely to succeed if you have financial assistance. Please be sure to visit your financial aid office right away and don't forget—you can't receive grants, loans, scholarships, or paychecks without applying.

Chapter 6

Decide on a Major that's Right for You

ANITA

"I've always been drawn to literature and writing and loved to read as a young girl, so I knew I'd major in English one day."

WHEN I FIRST started college in 2001, I wanted to be a nurse. When I went back to a new college in 2007, I planned to get an Administrative Secretary certificate and be done with it. Four years later, as a full-time student, I declared my major as Child Development. At the time, I wanted to become a preschool teacher. I did love the major and the classes I took were helpful to me as a future teacher and a parent. However, in 2012 I realized I've always truly been an English major. I love reading, I love writing, and that's who I am.

I should have known English would end up being my major. In second grade I had read *Charlotte's Web*, and then wrote the whole story down on paper. Yes, I plagiarized the entire book, but I was only in second grade so let's not be too judgmental toward my seven-year-old self. My teacher praised my efforts once she had taught me the importance of not taking other people's work. By sixth grade I was playing school with my best friend. Our teachers would donate leftover school papers for us to use, and we'd go all out with our imaginary classroom filled with invisible students. In grade school I also had an opportunity to help a second grade Vietnamese student learn

English. Once a week I went to visit her and brought along my most current Scholastic magazine. I would read to her and we did all the puzzles and activities together. I had fun while teaching her to read, write, and speak English. My good deeds didn't go unrecognized because at the end of the year I won a special tutoring award. That was a proud moment for sure.

I loved to read and write and I loved teaching—those two things I knew for certain. I just didn't realize those interests would lead to a career. Now I do. Once I chose the major that was right for me, as opposed to a major that might get me on the fast track to a career or pay a larger amount of money, college became a more enjoyable, fulfilling experience. I love what I do and hate missing class. Every discussion is fascinating; I jump right in and soak up knowledge.

Choosing your major may not be something you can do in five minutes or even five days. I've seen many people in college—both traditional and nontraditional students—change their majors. You may be 100% certain of your major, and if so, that's GREAT. Having a clear-cut goal is half the battle. However, many prospective students don't have a strong feeling about what they want to do in life. Some people are looking for a major that will help them land a good job, while others choose a major based strictly their interests. Consider the following ideas as you think about this decision:

1. **Don't decide before you start.** When you apply to either a two or a four-year school, you'll be prompted to choose a major, but you aren't required to do so. You can often select the "undecided" option.[4] Don't feel bad about waiting until you take a few classes to consider options. Once you get into this new academic life you'll be able to see what classes feel most important to you.

2. **Research majors at your college.** Find out what majors are popular, and why. While it may be a good choice to

---

4   Choosing a major is required when transferring from a community college to a university.

pick a popular major, you also have to consider class availability. Ask your peers about their majors and what they like about their selected areas of study. You'll find several resources on campus that can help you.

a. You can visit the **career center**, a place where the staff is devoted to helping students choose careers and find jobs. Who better to help you than people who are equipped with information about the career market?

b. Likewise, the **transfer center** is essential if you plan on moving to a university after community college. The transfer center is a great place to learn about your top university choices. In doing this, you will talk to various people about career availability and transfer opportunities. This doesn't mean you have to choose a major that makes the most money, but it allows you to weigh your options.

c. Last, if you have a few majors in mind, consult with a **major advisor**. These professors are selected by their respective departments to talk to students about the major. You can find out what's required to graduate, where you can transfer (if you plan to do so), what to expect at the next level (master's or Ph.D. programs), and what the career is like from the professors' experience.

3. **If you aren't going to transfer, don't finish your general education classes before you choose.** While I'm all about making this choice in your own time, I advise you not to wait until all your general education units are completed before you decide on a major. General education units are basic classes that make up the majority of your degree: math, science, English, speech, etc. Major-specific units are earned in your main subject, whatever that may be. Getting your general education units out of the way seems like a great idea, but then you'll find yourself with a few semesters that

only consist of your major subject. This can be exciting, overwhelming, or boring. For example, my friend Jessica was an English major and all she did was read and write for the final year of her degree. That may seem like a dream come true for the typical book nerd, but it can also become difficult. Instead, try to take a mixture of classes in the general education requirements and in your major. That way you're making progress in both areas, even before you decide.

4. **Don't choose a major because a friend or family member tells you to.** I'm sure you're your family members have your best interests at heart, but they aren't always right. I've actually met people who chose their initial major because someone else told them to do it. Yes, your family knows you, but it's crucial to make this choice yourself. After all, you're the one who'll do the work once you finish college, so please choose something you actually enjoy doing. If your family and friends offer advice, listen and consider, but don't feel obligated to follow in anyone's footsteps unless you truly want to be there.

5. **Shadow someone in a career that interests you.** If a friend or family member has a job that piques your interest, ask to shadow them for a few days to gain insight into that profession, including the stress level and working environment. If the shadowing goes well, this might be a good time to sign up for an intro class in a required subject for that particular job. If you can't shadow someone, ask that person to describe a typical day.

6. **On that note, don't choose a major based on the intro class.** While some majors are exclusive, many have intro classes that double as general education classes. Because of this fact, the classes are often a general overview of the field. Yes, you can get a glimpse into the major, but it isn't as representative as one would

hope. If an intro class interests you and you want to know more, try another class. After two classes you should have a better idea of what the major is like, thus allowing you to decide if it's right for you.

7. **Find your passion and run with it.** In order to choose a major you might to do what I did: Look back to your childhood, your teen years, and early twenties. What did you love? What did you dream of becoming when you grew up? If you already have a passion, find a way to incorporate it into college life. If you love children, try a few classes in the child development major. If you love math, try math, accounting, or statistics. You get the idea. I chose my major because I absolutely love to read, write, and teach. What better major for me than English?

8. **Don't be afraid to start again . . . and again.** I'd be lying if I told you I was one hundred percent certain I wanted to teach. Honestly, I've found myself researching other advanced degrees, like a doctorate in education or a second master's degree. What I do know is that we change and grow as we mature. If you find yourself halfway through a degree and realize your passion lies elsewhere, then run, don't walk, over to the advising center and talk to someone. You may be able to switch without losing too many your units, or you might be able to choose a new major and still get a minor in your previous major. My point is, don't feel the need to keep moving forward in a program that won't lead to an enjoyable career or won't help you support your family with a livable wage.

Choosing a major is essential and important on the road to success, but it doesn't have to be a quick decision and it needn't be final. You control your own college education. This is a huge investment you're making in your future—financial, mental, and emotional—so be sure you're satisfied with your choices.

Chapter 7

Build Relationships in College

Melissa

"Part of supporting myself also meant seeking help when I needed it. First, I made appointments to see my professors during office hours when I needed help. Secondly, I made a friend—a fellow college mom who knew the ins and outs of college and helped tremendously with the intangible things."

IF YOU PLAN on attending college only to get an education, you could miss one of the greatest benefits of college: relationships. No one graduates without the support of professors, staff, mentors, and peers. The connections you make during these crucial years can enrich your life and serve you throughout your career.

You have the chance to build four types of relationships while attending college: professors, support staff, peers, and mentors.

Communicate with Your Professors

Instructors are gatekeepers to the college experience—and graduation. You may not like all your professors and some of them won't be outstanding teachers, but YOU are still responsible for taking control of your grades and working with each professor to attain the best possible outcome for yourself.

I've built relationships with many professors while pursuing my education and I could tell you countless stories where communication was a key element. One such example is the communication between my grammar professor and me. I struggled with coursework during my final semester because of a difficult pregnancy. I had three options: attend class and suffer physically, drop out and defer graduation until the fall, or talk to my professor about working together to make his class possible, despite my situation. After spending quite a few years in college I knew the best option and wasted no time connecting with him.

I sent him an email explaining I'd been placed on limited activities pending my next ultrasound exam. He responded within 24 hours, offering to help me reach the finish line with a passing grade. That was such a reassuring message—and the communication didn't stop with him. Just one month from graduation I was able to work completely from home with my other professors. Had I not chosen to communicate I might have forfeited all my classes and hard work.

When I began a graduate program the same week I gave birth to my fourth child via C-section, I had to tell my professors I wouldn't be physically able to attend class for a few weeks. Once again I was overwhelmed by the kind attitude each professor showed and how easy it was to communicate with them. One professor in particular, Dr. Blaine, helped me by sending me the class syllabus far in advance, allowing me to read the text while recuperating at home. He was also more than happy to record class sessions while I was gone. By helping in these seemingly minor ways, he allowed me to be a member of the class from afar, instead of coming back during the fifth week with absolutely no idea what I was walking into—or worse, coming back too soon and suffering physical consequences. These small actions helped me not only prepare for class, but also stop worrying about my grades and stay occupied during the stressful postpartum period.

Though I've had great experiences, I know many students are flat-out afraid to approach professors. They rush to leave the classroom, hesitate to ask questions, and don't take advantage of office hours. Not getting to know each professor is one of the worst things you can do. I encourage you to reach out in person, by phone, e-mail, or office hours. Stand out from the pack and make yourself visible, in a good way, without being overly pushy.

Professors like to know you're serious about your education. If you make yourself known during office hours, they're more likely to help you above and beyond what you might expect. Don't be led to believe professors don't care about your education, because I know that 99% of them do care. Here are some tips on communicating with your professors.

1. **Know each professor's office hours.** Professors hold office hours for a reason—to meet one-on-one with students and discuss issues that occur. However, don't decide to randomly drop in on a professor during "off" hours. Be respectful of their time.

2. **Don't wait until the last ten minutes** of office hours to get help. If you have a job, during the final ten minutes before you clock out, don't you kind of mentally check out? And so it is with your professor. And what if your issue ends up being complicated? Be respectful and courteous by allowing sufficient time to address your concerns or questions.

3. **Be prepared when you go into office hours.** Know what you want to ask, have your book or papers ready, and bring a notepad. When you appear to be an organized and responsible person (even if deep down you feel chaotic), your professor will take note and remember.

4. **If you e-mail your professor, do so with professionalism.** Your professor may be friendly but that doesn't mean you are BFF's. When e-mailing, address each instructor

as he or she asked you to in class. Some professors don't like being called by their first names. At the beginning of your message, state which class you're in (they often have four to five classes with 30 students each), and then ask a brief question or state your concerns. Close the e-mail with a "thank you" or another salutation like "respectfully" instead of just signing your name. You want to build a reputation with your professor as a serious, dedicated, and professional student. One of my previous professors told me she had a student simply write, "read it" on an e-mail heading. Totally rude—don't do it!

5. **When you have to miss class, be sure to contact your professor.** E-mailing or calling is enough. You don't have to be detailed, but you can briefly share that your child is ill, you have to go to the emergency room, etc. Ask if you may attend an alternate class and ask about any homework. While most students miss a class, being a parent definitely raises the likeliness of having to be absent from time to time. Never ask if you missed something important—that question minimizes the work a professor puts into each class session. Did you miss anything important? Yes, you missed the entire class. (If you really are concerned, ask your classmates).

6. **Tell your professors you're a parent.** Most professors are parents themselves, or have taught hundreds of students who are parents. They understand you have an extra burden to carry and, most of the time, they'll work with you. For example, one of my professors asked that everyone turn off their phones during class—except parents who needed to be reached in case of emergency. Since my professor knew beforehand I had three children (and one with a special need), she expected my phone to be on. On the other hand, don't expect special privileges just because you're a parent.

Letting your professors know you're a parent simply allows them to understand you a bit more, but they can't help you if you don't communicate.

7. **Don't be embarrassed to ask for help.** Being a mom doesn't automatically make you super human or all-knowing (although our younger kids may think so). If you need help and are willing to say so, your professors will be happy to help. This is especially important for moms who are just returning to college or entering for the first time. For some reason we feel a major lack of confidence over being different. However, professors run into all types of people from various backgrounds. On the other hand, don't act helpless or expect to get out of working hard. Study the syllabus—that's your roadmap to getting an A in class. Professors will be peeved if you ask a question that's answered in the syllabus.

8. **Be a great student.** Pay attention in class and fully participate. Professors notice and respect students who look them in the eye, take notes, do the reading, attend every class, and speak up during class discussions. They're less likely to help if they sense you're trying to get out of doing the work.

Effectively communicating with professors is a vital part of your college experience. When you take time to do this with respect and courtesy, you will build relationships that may lead to later benefits, such as letters of recommendation, references, friendships, and mentoring. So don't be shy. Get to know your professors and seek out their expertise.

Form Friendships

When I first started college I kept to myself and avoided other students, both traditional and nontraditional. First of all, I didn't think it would work out for me, as a mom, to have friends like the traditional, everyday students. Second, I felt intimidated by everyone around me. This wasn't their fault, of course, but my own—and it links back to the "believe in yourself" concept from Chapter 1. I had zero confidence and almost felt guilty for wanting to learn and advance my education. However, before long I got to know many other students—some who were just like me, and others who were traditional. Both groups of friends became an integral part of my journey.

You need to make friends. The diversity, relationships, and connections you experience with your peers will give you support to manage your life when things get tough, as well as open your eyes to opportunities. These may be connections you'll keep for the rest of your life. You may find that friends will . . .

- Help you with difficult subjects.
- Add fun and zest to your college experience.
- Alert you to new opportunities, such as jobs, internships, and scholarships.
- Motivate you to stay in school.
- Broaden your perspective of life.

One friend in particular pulled me through a difficult time and, despite being a generation apart, our friendship blossomed through shared experience on an advisory board. Max and I started as acquaintances, but soon became good friends even though our college experiences were completely different. We were both chosen as members of the Pearson Student Advisory Board the year I transferred to Cal State Fullerton. When I first met Max he was a 20 year-old Texan with wispy, chocolate brown hair and a bright smile. He was reserved but friendly and we clicked almost immediately. Our friendship blossomed over the course of the year we worked together; every time we reunited, it felt as if no time had passed. Now Max is serving the people of West Africa, still wispy-haired, but a few years older and with a college degree under his belt. I guess you can say we survived college together, though not at the same school. And while he couldn't quite understand my experience as a mom (and I his), Max was an integral part of my college experience. Here's why:

1. **Max didn't judge me.** Not all traditional students are judging you; in fact most of them probably aren't. Sometimes we think every student who isn't a parent is giving us the stare of judgment when we walk into a classroom. That is false. Having a traditional college friend like Max reminded me I was accepted on my college campus and in special organizations like the student advisory board.

2. **He never saw me as too old to be a colleague or friend.** Although I'm a decade older, Max never pointed that out. Why? Because he knew that age has nothing to do with friendship. Along with my other traditional student-friends Max truly made me feel like a normal student. I know you may be shaking your head at my desire to fit in, but I want to be accepted and I like being part of the group. I suggest you consider that mindset also, because you'll assimilate better as a student and peer if you don't flaunt your differences.

3. **Max was a great supporter.** Max was always excited to see me succeed and I felt the same about him. Even though this book is for moms in college, Max wants to read it—he wants his own copy. He doesn't care at all that he isn't a mom and already finished college. His support for my dream means a lot to me.

4. **He was busy too!** One of the nice things about being friends with other college students is that you're all busy. Well, at least those who are serious about their grades. You'll enjoy having a friend who's also running around like a crazy person, trying to make projects, papers, and exams come together. While your mom-friends may also be super busy as parents, they won't understand your exact kind of college crazy. Your college friends totally get it.

You may discover your non-college friends (and family members) are a bit jealous of the new friendships. They may even ridicule you for being enthusiastic about college, making friends, and spending time on campus when not in class. I'm not saying you should ditch all your pre-college friends; I'm saying your life will be enriched if you find friends who may not be parents, full-time employees, or any number of variables, but still understand the struggles of college life.

Sure, you'll encounter a few barriers to friendship with traditional students: You live off campus while most other students live in dorms; you need to go home to your family; you're responsible for cooking, shopping, cleaning, and other activities around running a household. Still, you can overcome those differences and bridge the gap by reaching out to other students. With a little effort you can develop a friendship network that will help you succeed in college and beyond.

Become Allies with Other Moms in College

While building relationships with traditional students is important, I also encourage you to connect with other nontraditional students, especially moms. You may feel alone when you begin college, but remember that at least two million other moms just like you are enrolled in college—and some of them have to be on your campus. While we can apply all the attributes of friendship mentioned above, add to that another layer of support from fellow mothers in college. These relationships can keep you accountable and encouraged at the same time because these women understand the burdens you carry along with your heavy backpack.

Taking time to connect with other moms will help you answer questions like, "Who can I study with?" and "Does anyone know where there's a changing table on campus?" You might even form a playgroup and find new friends for your kids. The mothers I met in college became my strongest allies as a student.

Where do you find these women? The best way to meet is through a parenting club, an adult re-entry center, a counseling center, or maybe in a class. Joining workshops and seminars offered by these various clubs and offices will help you connect to others. If a group for parents doesn't exist on your campus, consider starting one yourself. That will be a perfect way to meet new people, expand your leadership skills, and enhance your resume.

Find a Mentor

A mentor is a special person in your life who encourages you to BE more, expects you to DO more, and shows you what can be achieved. This person sets an example and gives invaluable advice that only comes from experience.

During my first year as a fulltime community college student, I wasn't sure what I wanted from college. Feeling alone and vulnerable, I had a vague plan for teaching preschool. I spent my first two semesters focusing on that goal, which would mean I didn't need a four-year university. Then I met a woman who changed my life.

My first mentor, Dr. McCormick, didn't impress me in a positive way at first. When I tell people I left her first English class session with a migraine they think I'm kidding, but I'm serious. She was overwhelming to the point that I loved and hated her after that first two-hour meeting. I went to my honors adviser in a panic and told her I couldn't handle the class, but she said, "You can do it." So, I stayed.

What was so difficult—this was an English class, right? Plus, it was in my major! Well, Dr. McCormick didn't teach like the other instructors. First, she assigned difficult reading material that was challenging to grasp—followed by quizzes. I failed one quiz and received a C on all but two others. I tried to be mad at her, but it was my own fault because I didn't read the text thoroughly, nor did I practice critical thinking and good study habits. The same level of difficulty was present in her essay assignments. Though we sometimes felt as though she thought we couldn't succeed, her assignments told me I had the ability to read deep philosophical and political literature. Dr. McCormick assigned such readings as *Civil Disobedience* by Henry D. Thoreau and *The Social Contract* by Rousseau. She began the class with Plato's *Allegory of the Cave* and ended with Ursula K. Le Guin's, The *Ones Who Walk Away from Omelas.* Within these texts she expected us to find evidence and argue a side regarding matters of social justice—something none of us had done before. And she didn't accept weak arguments. Instead, Dr. McCormick pushed until you hit a new level of understanding. And I did. She was teaching us the art of critical thinking.

While I continued leaving the class with migraines from stress, I soon realized I loved how Dr. McCormick taught. She managed to be scary, intelligent, funny, and serious all at the same time. And while her classroom persona was spirited and fast-paced, the mentor I came to know in her office was a woman who genuinely cared about my education and development as a person. In particular, Dr. McCormick pushed me to keep going even when I failed. By giving me hope she also gave me the freedom to view myself as she saw me: capable, smart, confident, and persistent. Because of my mentor's influence, I soared.

While I knew Dr. McCormick would always be an important person in my life, when I transferred from Mt. SAC to Cal State Fullerton, I needed to find another mentor. This process didn't take long, as I soon met Dr. Caldwell, a professor many students believe is an absolute saint. I first met Dr. Caldwell in her Chaucer class, having already heard the legends about her challenging courses. I was initially terrified, but in time at all I realized Dr. Caldwell was a true gem, a professor I wanted on my side. So I asked her to be my mentor, and of course she said yes. Dr. Caldwell renewed my passion to teach, through her genuine belief in my ability to inspire students. She told me when I was being ridiculous by taking on too many projects, and she comforted me during one of the darkest times in my education at CSUF.

I'm sharing these life lessons so you can see how deeply these mentors impacted my life. Through both of these amazing women I've learned the importance of education and the value that mentorship adds to both the student and mentor. Finding a mentor is one of the wisest choices you can make—and it doesn't have to be difficult. If you're an older student you may think you don't need help, but everyone can use career guidance. Why?

- *You will have moments of weakness and you may already lack confidence or motivation.*

My mentors empowered me. Sometimes they did so without words, and sometimes they did it with more words than I wanted to hear. The truth may hurt, but I respect anyone who's willing to stand up and be honest instead of sugar coating things for people. Thanks to my first mentor, I no longer thought of myself as stupid. Before that first English class with Dr. McCormick, I had no confidence, little self-worth, and not an iota of belief I could ever receive a bachelor's or master's degree. You need mentors who will empower you while also being honest. They will help you keep your feet on the ground while pursuing your dreams.

- *You are more than a mom, and you're allowed to dream, set goals and achieve those goals.*

My mentors encouraged me to dream. I once believed being a mother would occupy my entire life. I thought I was no longer allowed to have dreams of my own or set personal goals. Anything and everything had to be for my children. Dr. McCormick blew that myth out of my mind and helped me choose a new direction for my life. Having goals and dreams for yourself won't make you a bad mom. In fact, it can make you an even better parent. I learned that from both of my mentors.

- *Having someone cheer you on is never a bad thing.*

My mentors are in my corner. After earning A's in all three of Dr. McCormick's classes (and let me tell you getting an A from her is NOT easy), and successfully graduating and transferring, I had someone behind me who knew the college system, knew me well enough to recommend me for jobs, scholarships, and special programs—and lastly, someone who would always be in my corner and believe in me when I didn't believe in myself. That kind of relationship is irreplaceable. Because of my wall-ripping, truth telling, challenging, inspiring, motivating, and supportive mentors, I can promise your college experience will be SO much better if you connect with a role model.

- *We all need career help and advice.*

Mentors can help with your career. You should plan to stay in touch with your mentors after you graduate, especially during your job search and when you enter the workplace. This will probably be through emails and an occasional phone call or greeting card as you navigate new terrain in the professional world.

How do you find a mentor?

1. **A mentor in your major subject:** This person can be fairly easy to find if you think about the classes you've taken and which professors influenced you the most. Did a certain professor take extra time with you and engage with you outside of class? Did he/she connect with you differently than other professors by showing concern not only for your academics, but your wellbeing in general? This person may be perfect.

2. **The counseling mentor.** If you haven't already seen an academic counselor, you should do so. Not only do counselors know what it takes for success in college, many of them take a personal interest in helping

students make the most of their education. They know what classes you should and shouldn't take; they probably even know what days are better for parking! If you've seen a counselor on a regular basis, consider this person a mentor.

3. **The professor mentor.** This professor, unlike the first, doesn't have to be in your major to know the challenges of being a college student. Many professors outside my major were capable and willing to be my mentor, offering support in various areas of my life. An inspirational professor doesn't have to be in your major in order to know who you are. If you know a professor whose class you enjoyed, that person might be a good option.

4. **A nontraditional student mentor.** This mentor can be a professor, counselor, administrator, or someone outside of college who went through an experience similar to yours. If you know someone who succeeded in college as a mom (or dad), ask about the experience. You will learn a lot.

5. **The career mentor.** This mentor may be a bit harder to reach, but if you have a chance to connect with someone in your desired field or with an organization you'd like to work for, please connect with them. What better way to look inside your desired career than by communicating with someone who's already there? You can make contact with these people at guest lectures, extracurricular activities, and by doing internships.

Some colleges allow students to sign up with mentors online. Ask your academic counselor about this. Once you do find a possible mentor and establish a relationship, simply ask. Most people will be delighted to help, because mentoring a student who wants to succeed and takes your advice is one of the best feelings in the world.

When you establish a relationship, don't forget to say, "Thank you!" Show your appreciation with thoughtful gestures, like sending a card now and then. Don't drop a mentor when you get what you want. Nothing is more valuable than the time a person gives you. Respect that.

Networking

In today's job market getting a degree isn't enough to start your career. Networking is such a crucial part of college that entire books are written on the subject. You need to start building a network and personal brand long before you graduate.

What does this mean? First, a personal brand is basically marketing yourself. You begin doing this online through sites such as LinkedIn, About.me, and so on. You are creating a professional image to share your great qualities with the world. Networking means taking your personal brand and connecting with others who are already employed in your field or have the same career interests. Your network might include:

- Family, friends, and acquaintances,
- Classmates, both older and younger,
- Alumni from your school,
- Professional organizations (you can join as a student),
- Academic organizations,
- Fraternities and sororities,
- Religious groups.

Whether you realize it or not, you've been networking your whole life. Starting with preschool, you forged relationships with classmates. At some point you took an interest in a friend's life, shared your life with that person, and found a way to build mutual trust and respect. Without even thinking about it, you learned to convince other people that you are respectable, honest, friendly, exciting, and loyal.

You may be saying, "But I don't want to manipulate people!" We've all had classmates or coworkers who were called brown-nosers and these folks are usually easy to spot. Manipulation means using people for your own purposes with no regard for their needs and feelings. *You* will not be doing that. You'll be establishing relationships that may last for years and will benefit everyone involved.

How do you network if you spend half your life changing diapers? Simple. Start with your campus career center. After you learn all you can from the career center, seek out clubs that align with your career goals. Examples include the Pre-Dental Society for those seeking to earn a degree in dentistry, or the Teaching Writing Club for students like me who are preparing to teach college English (or even 7-12th grades). Additionally, you can join honor societies, either related to your major or not.

Also connect with professionals who come to campus for guest lectures. Introduce yourself and ask if you can visit their workplace. Some of your professors may be moonlighting from companies they work for. If that's the case, having one of these professors for a mentor might help you network into a job after graduation. As you build your network one person at a time, people will call you when they see an internship or job pop up that reminds them of you. This is the hidden job market—and you can tap into it.

Do something every day to maintain the networks you have in place and add new people. Over time, as you nurture these relationships, they will show value when you need them the most. Here's an example of how network might work for you:

Your friend Kylee desperately needs a job on campus and you've cultivated a friendship with the nice administrative assistant for one of your favorite professors. You know this woman needs someone to help with filing, so you recommend Kylee and she gets a job that allows her to stay in school. A year later when you graduate and begin your own job search, you remember Kylee's dad works in your field. Kylee puts in a good word for you and her dad finds you a job in his company. In that position you're able to help other new graduates from your school. Everyone in this scenario benefits from your networking skills.

As you can see, networking goes way beyond Facebook, Twitter, and texting. The secret to moving seamlessly from college to a great job (while bypassing entry level positions) lies with the people you meet in college and the people you already know. They will change your life.

Networking and branding may be a stretch for you, especially if you're running scared in college, but I can't emphasize enough the importance of these tools for success. Networking and creating a personal brand are why I was appointed to the Pearson Student Advisory Board; the reason I won scholarships; and why I've had people recommend me for campus jobs. Keep an open mind, be brave, and head over to the career center to get started.

Chapter 8

Get Involved

CHARLENE

"Participation in Phi Theta Kappa was a driving force to keep me in college and helped build my confidence in myself and my abilities. Campus activities helped me form one of my strongest support systems."

BY NOW YOU may be saying, "Duh! How am I supposed to fit extra stuff into my life when I have kids and classes? I'm already overwhelmed!"

I agree—the playing field isn't even for parents who are students. The temptation is to rush onto campus, attend one or two classes, and hurry back to our "real world" of work and parenting. But I'm asking you to think long term. The extra time you spend on campus today can lead to a better career and a new life for you and your family. You are not frittering away time—you're building your future.

As I look back on my undergraduate career, failing to be more involved on campus is a major regret. I didn't realize this was something I could manage as a mom in college. While I attended a few events such as music showcases, I didn't bother spending much time on campus after classes. I felt that joining clubs wasn't my place because those activities would take time away from my family. Plus, when I started college I didn't believe I should actually enjoy the experience.

I was so wrong. During my second fulltime semester at community college I joined Phi Theta Kappa, an international community college honor society. I didn't get the purpose right off the bat, but liked the idea of belonging to an honor society. However, a few months after being inducted I was able to start my own service event. My event went well, not only raising money for breast cancer awareness, but also having a large group of students walk the 5K event. I was proud of myself for accomplishing those goals. The best part of the event was being able to involve my family. Not only did I walk, but so did my son Matthew. I had a chance to educate him about breast cancer while also exposing him to a community of service-driven college students.

Soon afterward I found myself being honored with a state award as a Phi Theta Kappa student. Me? Award-winning? That couldn't be MY life! But it was, and my family was proud of me, especially my young children, who beamed with pride when I brought home my medallion.

Since that experience I opened my mind to the idea that it's okay to be involved and enjoy myself. I participated in other clubs, campus events, and an academic conference. I even stepped up to be the founding president of a nontraditional student honor society, knowing such a society would be important to students just like me—and like you. Because my involvement benefited me so greatly (without taking much time away from my family), I want to explain different options and give you reasons to consider getting involved yourself.

Clubs and Organizations

College clubs come in all shapes and sizes. To be honest, attending a Join a Club event can feel a bit overwhelming because you'll see dozens, even hundreds, of groups to choose from. Nevertheless, attending this event is a great way to meet club officers and window shop for a club. Sometimes clubs exist for parents in college, and if you find one on your campus, I recommend joining. Other clubs may speak to your interests elsewhere, such as your major or hobbies. You can find anything from faith-based clubs, identity-based clubs, to a creative writing club. But why join a particular group? Here are a few reasons to join:

1. **Personal Growth.** Yes, you're a mom in college and you may even be an older mom, but that doesn't mean you don't have room to grow. You can learn a lot about yourself and gain personal growth by joining a club that focuses on something new and challenging.

2. **Leadership Opportunities.** This can be connected to personal growth as well. Now, I'm not saying you have to be a founding president if you don't want that, but you'll probably have the opportunity to lead in various ways. Other positions include event planning, fundraising, secretary, treasurer, and social media coordinator. If you want to help, consider your skills and inquire about holding a position. You can gain leadership skills without holding an office by getting involved in events throughout the year. You might even decide to create your own event. These leadership opportunities make great resume enhancers. It's already impressive to be a mom in college, but a mom in college who takes on a leadership role? That shows initiative and dedication, both important traits when applying for jobs.

3. **Volunteering and/or Community Service.** Here comes that time thing again, right? No. Community service events are fairly inclusive, so if finding a baby sitter for your six-year-old isn't easy he or she might be able to join in. Some events include helping at animal shelters, serving meals, collecting canned goods, or collecting trash around the community. What better way to set an example for your children than by reaching out to your community? Not only are you helping people, you're influencing your children to do the same. That is a win-win situation.

Honors Programs

I know you're out there! Yes, you—the mom with the 3.5 or higher GPA who's a born overachiever and has recurring nightmares about getting a C on a single paper. Even though you have a fantastic GPA, part of you still thinks either:

- *It's a fluke; I'm not really that smart. (Hello, imposter syndrome!)*

- *I won't fit in with other students in the honors program because I'm too old, boring, out of touch, or mom-ish.*

Both of these assumptions are false. As a mom in college who's been part of the honors program at both a community college and a university, I want to list a few reasons why you should definitely join the honors program if your campus has one:

1. **Support, support, support.** Did I mention support? While both my colleges offered GREAT support services, I found the most (and best) encouragement in the honors center/department. The adviser understands me because she deals exclusively with honors students. You know the type: obsessed about our grades, panicking over registration dates, etc. She gets it. She's a great counselor and, because there are fewer honors students than regular students seen by other advisers, she had time to get to know me—and that made a huge difference. I am confident most honors programs are the same. As a student and a mom in college, you will feel supported.

2. **Classes.** Plain and simple, honors classes usually have a smaller student to faculty ratio. I don't know about you, but the idea of only 10 to 20 students in one class is quite nice. This is especially true for speech and communications classes, math, and science. Smaller honors classes give both you and the professor time to get to know each other and also let students connect

with one another and have a voice during class. Not only are the classes smaller, they usually include elements you won't find in the typical college class.

3. **Scholarship opportunities and recognition.** School is expensive. Even if you get financial aid, it won't cover everything and you may need to take out loans. As a member of the honors program you may be eligible for scholarships exclusive to those in the program. Even if you don't win a scholarship you can still be recognized and that recognition may lead to later scholarships and opportunities. For example, I was selected as a Phi Theta Kappa All California Academic Team member, which in turn opened many doors and windows for me. Sometimes non-monetary awards can lead to greater things down the road.

4. **Transfer opportunities.** Transferring isn't easy and is especially competitive in certain regions of the country. Being an honors student can help you transfer, because honors centers have agreements with 4-year college honors programs and the staff often keeps in direct contact with the honors program on the transfer campus.

5. **Friends/Peer Support.** I know some of you are thinking, "I don't have time for friends" or "I don't need friends," but once you spend a certain amount of time on campus you'll just end up making friends. Even if you're older or have five kids, having a friend or two on campus is a great thing. Nobody should feel alone on the academic journey and there's no better place to find friends than in the honors center.

Academic Conferences and Events

A few years ago you wouldn't ever find me at a writer's day, an academic conference, or any event in the academic world. As a nontraditional, older mom in college, I felt I didn't belong in in such activities. Then, after being rejected by a few literary magazines and other essay contests, I actually found a bit of confidence and submitted poems to the Mt. San Antonio College Writers Day contest. To my surprise, I won 3rd place in poetry! Until that time I'd never shared my poetry, so this was scary for me. However, realizing other people liked my writing changed my perspective. Waiting for the event was hard on my nerves, but when the big day arrived, the head of the program found a good session for me to join and I was surprised by the other people in the room: Young and not-so-young, all in one room listening to an incredibly funny author speak. I loved it. Then came the awards ceremony. While recognition is fun, I'm never a fan of being in the literal spotlight. Nevertheless, receiving the award was a great experience and the published collection that included my poem just topped it off.

I had the honor, and pleasure, of submitting my abstract to SCCUR — Southern California Conference for Undergraduate Research, in my junior year. Now, I don't know if you know, but many of these undergraduate conferences are filled heavily with STEM fields (science, technology, engineering, math), but most try to include all areas of study. However, usually the English/Literature students choose to do an oral presentation. While it was ambitious and my adviser told me I might not be accepted, I chose to submit my abstract from a literary research assignment based on the works of Jane Austen, with the intent to create an academic poster. An academic poster is a form of research presentation where the scholar creates a visual representation of her research. Most posters are from science-based courses, but slowly the Humanities are adding to this form of academic scholarship. Once created, the scholar attends a poster session with his or her peers and stands next to the poster answering questions from conference attendees about the topic. If you aren't comfortable with presenting research in the form of a speech, this is a great alternative because it's normally a one-on-one conversation or a few people.

As the days crept closer to the Day of Decision and many of my friends had been contacted and asked to revise their abstracts, I was certain I wouldn't be accepted. However, much to my surprise, I was accepted without need for revision.

So I attended the conference and waited for my poster session (an hour-and-a-half time slot). After attending the keynote, I waited in the hall for visitors. Seriously, I thought maybe two people would stop, but several people stopped by and asked great questions. Some took pictures of my poster. Afterward I found out a professor from another university saw my poster and contacted my adviser to tell her how nice it was. My poster! Me, a 30-something, mom of three attended this amazing conference among so many bright and talented students. It was fantastic. Oh, and I was the ONLY English poster presentation among the three poster sessions—I went against the grain and it felt GOOD!

So, what does this have to do with you? I'm sharing this story because I know you can do something similar. These conferences didn't take a large portion of my time, and yet they benefited me so much. Don't say, "This isn't for me!" until you've at least tried. You truly don't know whether you like something until you try. And your ideas are just as bright as the traditional student next to you. So, when opportunities like these that present themselves—embrace and enjoy them!

How do you connect with opportunities? First, by attending those "Join a Club" days I mentioned earlier. If you miss that event, you can search for clubs on your college website or contact the student life office. For the honors program, if you aren't invited after doing well, the best way to get in touch (or find) an honors program is through your academic counseling office, the school website, or by consulting with professors. Finally, if you'd like to attend an academic event, ask a faculty member. Don't stress out about the financial cost, because many colleges offer financial support so you can get that experience. Now go out there and get involved!

Volunteering and Internships

For almost any career path you choose, internships and volunteer work will help you gain experience and make valuable contacts before graduation. Being a volunteer means working without pay or college credit, but you gain intangible benefits and real life experience. Also, volunteering is an outstanding way to influence your children, showing them the value and importance of giving without receiving. An internship is a working position, usually without pay, but most academic internships offer college credit. Some college majors require volunteer work and/or internships, because these experiences help you become more involved in your college community and the community at large. Competition is fierce for the best internships, so plan ahead. Visit the career center or check out your college's online job board. You will probably find volunteer experiences through the same channels, but can also seek your own, depending on your major. Either way, these two experience-gaining positions will help complete your college experience while also building your resume. Internships offer the following advantages:

- Earn college credit
- Fulfill degree requirements
- Learn how to apply academic courses to the professional world
- "Test drive" a profession to see if you truly like it
- Uncover new talents
- Develop responsibility and new, transferable skills
- Gain possible full-time employment at your internship site
- Make professional contacts in your field of study.

Researching and applying for these forms of involvement can be time consuming, but the benefits you'll receive are well worth your time. You don't have to do everything, but you should try to do something. Even committing one hour a week to a club is great. Find a club, honor society, internship, or volunteer opportunity that feels right for you, and then go for it!

Chapter 9:

Push Through the Road Blocks

TAMIKA

"My advice to you is this: Keep striving for your dreams and desires even if life's challenges derail you from your chosen path. Life is too short to be filled with regret. Nothing is more gratifying than accomplishing a goal you set for yourself, no matter how big or small."

DURING THE FIRST week of my first semester after transferring to Cal State Fullerton, I experienced one of the most challenging issues of my college career. My husband, who has a compromised immune system due to a rare blood disorder called hereditary spherocytosis, became very ill. While most people overcome pneumonia with a round of antibiotics, his blood disorder left him without a spleen at the age of five, which makes him vulnerable to life-threatening infections. This time he ended up with an advanced infection in the lining of his left lung, known as empyema. Within a week he went from "a little sick" to a hospital admission for surgery. We battled insurance issues as we were well below the poverty line and had applied for state insurance, but they took their time approving our family. Because of this delay, the local hospital couldn't transfer him to a better hospital. I would not stand for this. No matter who you are, where you are from, and how much (or little) money you make, you should receive lifesaving care as needed. I spoke to state insurance agents for two days, constantly making myself known, and within three days my husband's insurance was approved, the surgery was done, and his slow road to recovery began. And I do mean *slow*.

This ordeal left me questioning what to do about school. Should I completely drop out? Should I stay on campus full time? Ultimately I decided it would be best to drop all three of my on-campus courses and spend the semester solely online. This went well for two classes, but I wasn't able to secure a third. However, the one campus class I kept was my first literature course (in my major) and the professor, Dr. Dalley, was incredibly understanding toward my situation. As a mother of three and wife herself, she was concerned for me and my husband. Her attitude made a huge difference. Even though life changed for my family, I was able to remain in school. Often while on campus my mind wasn't on schoolwork, but on worries about my husband: Was he lonely? Did he need me to bring anything? Did something happen while I was in class? I was terrified of losing him—of having my children lose their father and the world lose such a wonderful, funny man.

For the first month of school I spent little time focusing on schoolwork, but once David started to heal and came home the stress level improved. I completed that first transfer semester with three A's and a B, which left me astounded by my own resilience. I also felt great relief that I survived alongside my husband. What did I learn? *Life happens.* And as you know, it happens every day regardless of plans you may have. You can't give up. You MUST keep moving forward, even in the face of adversity. Difficult times will push against you more often than you can imagine, but you have the ability to keep going, even if you take baby steps along the way.

During my time in college I overcame many hurdles: guilt about not spending time with my kids, missing classes due to illnesses, failing exams, having to apply for food stamps, and a new pregnancy. I know you'll face some of these same challenges, plus others that are unique to your situation. I won't be able to discuss every type of roadblock, but I hope this chapter will show how attitude and perseverance can help overcome nearly every obstacle you might face.

Health Issues

Anyone who has children or works with them knows that illness can spread like wildfire. As a young mother I wasn't aware of this until my oldest son went to kindergarten. That kid caught everything! Since then, I've had to miss class more than once to care for a sick child. Health issues come in all shapes and sizes: you, your children, your spouse, and other family members may experience sickness and accidents. Yes, we know people get colds and flu and boo-boos, but don't they always seem to happen at the absolute worst times? It's never during the winter, spring, or summer break, but right smack dab in the middle of the semester. I learned to do everything in my power to prevent illnesses, and when that wasn't possible I communicated with my professors. Here are some options to help get you through illnesses while in college.

Prevention: Take care of yourself and practice good hygiene, while also teaching your children to do the same. The best thing you can do for your children is to teach and encourage them to wash their hands often and cover their sneezes and coughs. I know this doesn't always keep everyone healthy, but it can help. Another way to help prevent illness is to eat healthy, exercise, and take a multivitamin. That may seem like common sense, but in the middle of a crazy semester those three things can be pushed aside or forgotten. Do your best to schedule at least thirty minutes of cardio every day — doing something that gets your blood flowing. With that, be mindful of what you put into your belly. Junk food and heavy, high carb meals aren't the best way to stay healthy. Instead, make sure to include a variety of fruits and vegetables in your meals, and eat whole grains. You also need to pay attention to your water intake, because hydration can help prevent illness.

Don't overlook flu shots and other vaccines for yourself and your family. Some college healthcare centers offer free flu shots. Also, avoid skipping sleep in order to study. Your body needs time to recuperate from your busy days, so allow time to rest. Lastly, avoid unhealthy coping mechanisms like binge eating and consuming alcohol. Overall, prevention may not always be possible, but adhering to some of these options will give you a head start when the flu bug is chasing you one week before finals.

My second piece of advice, focused on the already-sick college mom, is to communicate with your professors. Call or email your professor as soon as you know the illness is going to keep you away from class. While many professors remain strict with their attendance policies, they also know there are some things you can't control. Going to the beach instead of class? Not so good. But going to the hospital while your husband is in the operating room? That's a legitimate reason to miss class. If the problem is ongoing, don't just contact your professor once. Keep the lines of communication open and you'll be surprised how accommodating some professors will be. Also, take the time to contact a classmate so can borrow class notes. It's a good idea to meet one or two classmates the first or second day of class and exchange numbers and email addresses. Having those notes may be your only insight into what you missed while dealing with an illness. (For a complete list of tips for communicating with your professor, visit Chapter Seven).

Pregnancy

I began writing this section during the first trimester of pregnancy with my fourth child. We had no intention of having another child, yet there I was—pregnant. As a firm believer that every child is born with a purpose, I faced my final semester prepared to follow the advice I'm about to give you. As if being a college student isn't stressful enough, being a pregnant college student is an entirely different ball game. Many women, both traditional and nontraditional students, struggle with pregnancy while attending college. From morning sickness (or all-day sickness as I like to call it) to swollen feet and tummies, to pure exhaustion, it's just not pretty! That's why many women who end up pregnant while working on their education will drop out of college either temporarily or permanently. I completely understand this. I faced the first week of my final semester terrified I wouldn't get through it because of between being sick all day and tiredness. But then I learned of a law that's quite valuable to the pregnant college student. I suspect most pregnant college students don't realize their rights are protected through Title IX (Education Amendments of 1972)[5]. If you are a pregnant woman in college, here are five things you should know:

1. Your college is not allowed to discriminate against you based on marital status, or if your condition changes due to childbirth, false pregnancy, or recovery from such conditions. What does this mean? If you're single and pregnant the school can't withhold any benefits or services they would offer a woman who is married and pregnant. It also means the school cannot change any decisions they make about your record on account of your condition.

2. Schools are required to treat pregnant women as they treat others. Medical benefits and related services are to be provided to pregnant students in the same manner as services provided to students with "other temporary disabilities." This can be a crucial part of college success, because if you don't have accessible healthcare and your college denies you services, you risk illness and complications that will not only harm you, but affect your college career as well. You are also entitled to receive services like at-home tutoring if your college

5   https://www2.ed.gov/about/offices/list/ocr/docs/dcl-know-rights-201306-title-ix. html

makes similar accommodations for those with other temporary disabilities. This may include special seating in the classroom for when your tummy starts to grow.

3. A pregnant student can be granted a leave of absence for as long as it is medically necessary and at the conclusion of her leave must be allowed to resume the status she held when the leave began. This, in my opinion, is one of the most important clauses. You cannot have absence due to your pregnancy held against you even if a professor has an attendance policy in place. This also means that your professor cannot adjust your grade on account of absences related to your pregnancy. However, you do need to provide documentation of your pregnancy in order to ease this process. Furthermore, if you were in good standing before you had to leave school on account of your condition, your status can't be lowered during that time. If you have a professor who isn't complying with this, you need to seek the aid of academic affairs.

4. Your professor and college must give you the opportunity to make up work you missed as a result of pregnancy, illness, or other disability. Regardless of whether the school tries to tell you it's up to each professor, federal law states the teacher must allow you to make up the work. Many people don't see pregnancy as a disability, but the fact remains that each and every pregnancy is different and many come with challenges. Colleges allow people with other conditions to make up work, so they must give you the same opportunity.

5. Please be sure to get proof of pregnancy from your doctor as soon as possible and visit the appropriate office, likely the disabled students center. From there you can start the process for receiving those benefits as one with a temporary disability.

You can do this! Don't think you must leave college because of your condition. Faculty, administration, and other students will support you during this challenging time in your life. Seek out resources on your campus and use them. Your education is yours and you have federal law on your side. Not only that, you have the power to be your own advocate. Continuing your education during pregnancy may not be easy, but it is possible.

Postpartum (or any form of) Depression

After the birth of my fourth child I desperately tried to avoid depression, but from previous experience I suspected it was happening. I stayed in denial for a month and tried to cope, but the truth became clear when I started feeling anxious about going to school, fearing the loss of my children, panicking over leaving them, sleeping all the time, and crying almost constantly; I knew I had to get help. I share this with you as either a precaution or an intervention, depending on your current situation. Postpartum depression, or depression in general, is debilitating and can change your life. I spent about five months of my first year in graduate school simply coping—or trying to cope. The day I left school crying, unable to face anyone or attend my next class, was the day I knew I had to get help.

If you believe you're depressed, I want to offer advice that might help you prevent some of the issues I faced:

1. **You are not alone.** If you take nothing else from this section of the book, let it be this message. Many college students suffer from anxiety and/or depression, so you are not unique on campus. A 2013 study showed that one third of college students had difficulty functioning due to depression and almost half reported overwhelming anxiety. And many women suffer from postpartum depression. Sixty to eighty percent of new moms report postpartum blues (sadness, anxiety, mood changes, etc.) that continue for a few weeks and eventually go away. Ten to twenty percent of new mothers experience lasting depression: despondency, anxiety, guilt, fatigue,

and even lack of feeling for the baby. These symptoms can occur any time during the first few months to one year after the birth.

2. **Do not be ashamed.** You are not defective, lazy, or a bad person because you're suffering. You did nothing wrong.

3. **Ask for help.** I mean this wholeheartedly because the only reason I succeeded that year of grad school was through the undying support of my professors and mentors. But I had to ask for the help I received. Their dedication to my success not only led to my achievements as a student, but also prompted me to finally seek medical help. Help is available. You don't have to give up on yourself or school.

4. **Seek professional help.** If you aren't sure where to start, visit the counseling center where certified counselors that can help you. Yes, even a mom in college! If that option doesn't exist or you'd rather visit your own doctor, then please do so. Depending on the type of doctor you're assigned to, you will either be referred elsewhere or the doctor will evaluate your situation and give recommendations based on your history.

5. **If you are prescribed medication, take it.** After two weeks my anti-depressant started to work and for the first time in five months I felt like myself again. Will you be on the medication forever? Probably not. Also, if you feel it's not working, talk to your doctor about trying another. Just be sure to give yourself (and the medication) two weeks to work. Furthermore, for your own safety, never stop taking an anti-depressant on your own; the effects can be dangerous to your health and wellbeing.

6. **Take. It. Easy.** I've said this in previous chapters, and I'm emphasizing it now. Don't overdo it. Even six months later your body is still recovering from the

rigors of creating and birthing a human, so you need time to recuperate. Even after you begin a medication, please still go easy on yourself.

Depression is an invisible, yet terrible illness and you will often feel alone through the struggle. However, you are never alone. Never forget how important you are.

Emotions: Getting through the Guilt

I've spent a significant amount of class time battling feelings of guilt over being away from my children. Although I know my children are safe at home or in childcare, my thoughts start to wander. And while I'm usually able to refocus my attention on the lecture, occasionally I begin questioning myself. It goes something like this: "Are they okay? I hope Mom picked them up from school on time. I wonder if they ate lunch. I hope no one fell off that trampoline in the back yard. Does my mom have a first aid kit? Do they miss me? Is this even worth my time? I could be home reading to them...or cooking them a nice meal...or taking them to the park. Will they grow up to remember me being gone so much, or being a hard working student? I wonder if their homework is finished...I wonder if any kids picked on them in school today. I feel like I'm abandoning my babies. I should go home early. No, I don't want to make a big deal of it. I miss my kids."

These are my personal worries, and I suspect most student moms have similar thoughts. It seems like a nice dose of guilt is packaged into every mother's DNA. However, this particular brand of worry is something we can and should overcome, for good reasons. While we always have our children on our minds, creating bad scenarios in our heads puts us in a fight-or-flight mindset: "I've got to leave now and save my babies!" When this happens, we bypass the logical part of our brains. The limbic (emotional/driven center) system goes on high alert, and we can no longer focus on the here and now or think realistic thoughts.

The way to cope with this anxiety is to name the issue, understand it, and then learn to "be" with your problem instead of trying to run home. I'll be the first to say it: My name is Dianna and I am dealing with guilt. But I can get through it—and so can you! Here are some positive things to remember when you're going through a guilt phase during class:

1. I'm here for a reason and I need to focus on the goals I set for myself. (I want to get an A in this class, or I want to graduate college, or I want to obtain a career in _____).

2. My children are safe. I selected a great person as a caregiver. I love my children and would not intentionally put them in harm's way. They will be okay. I can call or text later to make sure things are fine.

3. My children have a first-hand role model. They see me in college and want to be just like Mommy. I am proud of that.

4. It's okay to feel guilt. In fact, it's normal. However, the feeling of guilt is telling me a lie. I am not guilty of doing anything wrong.

5. Feeling guilty doesn't mean I'm a bad mom.

These are the things I learned to focus on when I start getting the urge to leave class in order to be with my kids.

Moms like us exist all over the world: Moms who work fulltime, go to school fulltime, or both. Being a mother is a tremendous role in life and one to be proud of, but you are more than a mom. You have desires and dreams and goals for yourself—and that's okay. Taking on the role of student doesn't make you less of a mother. I don't think my kids will look back on this time and resent me for attending classes a few hours each day. I think they'll remember this time and realize how hard I worked in school so they could have more opportunities in the future. I hope it helps show them the value of education.

Imposter Syndrome and Intimidation

Merriam-Webster's dictionary defines the word *intimidate* as "making someone timid or filling them with fear." And furthermore, it defines the root word *timid* as "fearful and hesitant." I'm defining these words because it's important for you to realize that fear is something most moms experience in college—even more so if you're an older mom. This ties into something psychologists now recognize as *imposter syndrome*: the feeling that you're unworthy and don't deserve success.

"I'm not smart enough to be in this class."

"I have no idea what I'm doing on campus."

"Everyone else is smarter and more prepared. They're probably laughing at me."

"I got an A in this class, but the professor probably made a mistake."

The American Psychological Association defines impostor syndrome as something that "occurs among high achievers who are unable to internalize and accept their success. They often attribute their accomplishments to luck rather than to ability, and fear that others will eventually unmask them as a fraud."

I experienced this when I received a state academic award and was celebrated among 80 of the best and brightest in California. The awards went to a few older students, but most were under 25. I felt incredibly intimidated by the brilliant students who obviously earned their spot. After reading their bios I knew I didn't belong and someone had made a mistake. I came face to face with the nasty lack-of-confidence monster.

I am old.

I am boring.

I am a mom.

I am not smart.

I can't say I've completely overcome these feelings, but I did find ten ways to help deal with them:

1. Immerse yourself in classes. Like adapting to cold water in a pool, the further you go in, the less cold it feels on your skin. Moving forward is the best way to move past insecurities. I threw myself fully into the public speaking class and it turned out to be one of my most successful classes. Just dive in!

2. You may think people don't like you — and maybe for some it's true — but overall, you have an opportunity to be a role model for other students. Sure you "did it backwards" by having your kids and THEN going to school, but trust me even young people will look upon your choices with respect and admiration. And trust me; many traditional students are probably intimidated by you, too.

3. Remember that everyone brings something to the table. Where traditional students have an easier time adapting because of their youthful spirit, you have something they don't: life experience. The best thing you can do is appreciate both worlds. And in turn you will find that others appreciate you too. A fellow mom in college chimed in on this issue and said, "One thing I like about being around younger students, as well as my teenage sons, is that you have a unique view of your own experience, plus the perspective of a younger, innovative generation."

4. Feeling a little scared can make you a better student. You'll want to always be prepared and make sure you understand what's going on around you.

5. Stop comparing yourself to others. You'll always meet people you believe are smarter, more gifted, and more attractive. Remember, each of us has problems and insecurities to deal with. Just be yourself and love who

you are. If you feel the need to compare yourself, do so only to the previous version of YOU. Compare where you were a year ago to where you are now. Gauge your success upon your own situation, allowing yourself room to learn and grow.

6. Know that you aren't alone with your feelings. Those traditional students who look cool and collected may be hiding feelings of insecurity. Don't let appearances fool you.

7. Stop expecting to be perfect. You aren't, and neither is the student in the seat next to you. As moms in college we are, most of the time, overachievers. In some ways we don't really have a choice because we have to overachieve in order to stay on top of our game, so to speak. And while there is NOTHING wrong with being an overachiever, there is something wrong with feeling like a failure if you don't get 100% on every assignment. If you were perfect you wouldn't need to be in school, would you? So try to cut yourself some slack in the perfection department.

8. Accept your success! Yes, we all get to the top with help from others (most times), but we chose to get there. Don't be afraid to celebrate your achievements. You aren't being cocky or overconfident—you're feeling proud of the hard work and struggle to get where you are. I suggest you compile of list of things you've achieved, from major to minor. Read this list when you feel insecure—and don't forget to celebrate your hard work with your family.

9. Talk with your mentor. I once spoke with a mentor about imposter syndrome. I slouched into her office feeling like a guilty criminal hiding from the authorities, only to find out she experienced the same thing. This incredibly brilliant woman I looked up to had faced the same issues of fear, anxiety, and intimidation. Your

mentor is likely to understand your feelings and can give you good advice.

10. Focus on the positive impact you have on others, not just your visible success. My mentor recently coached me through this issue. I don't feel like I am remarkable at all, I truly don't. I have a hard time accepting myself as successful or as making a contribution to society. She told me I shouldn't look at everything as something I'm doing for myself, but how it will impact others. As moms, our success will lead to great things for our children—and there's nothing fake about that.

You may continue feeling like an imposter for a long time, but remember that your journey is real, your experiences as a mom and a student are real, and the time and dedication you put forth are very real. Someday you'll look back and say, "Hey, I did that!"

Major Financial Setbacks

I've never lived above the poverty line until recently. While growing up, I was the only child of a single, intellectually disabled mother and we barely had money for food and clothing; certainly not for luxuries. This situation is increasingly common, though it has variations from one family to the next. In some situations, you might end up having to put college on hold for a while. However, you'll find assistance on and off campus that may get you through to that next job or financial resource. So what can you do?

1. Apply for temporary/transitional assistance. I spent my entire life in a low income family, most of which we survived without the help of welfare or food stamps. But while struggling to feed my own children I chose to do what was necessary so they would have nutritious meals. Many women feel ashamed of applying for assistance, even though in many places it's known as temporary or transitional assistance. If you find

yourself unable to afford food for your children or buy household essentials, please consider researching assistance in your city, county, and state. You're a college student working hard to improve yourself, and thus improve the future for your children. You are the ideal recipient.

2. Visit food banks and thrift stores. If you and your children are hungry, do not hesitate to look for a local food bank. They exist to help people in need. Thrift stores are great places to find good clothing for a low cost. This can be helpful if you need a classy interview outfit but can't afford something brand new.

3. Cut back on unnecessary spending. Do you have more cable channels than humanly necessary? How many gigabytes of data do you pay for on your cell phone? Do you need to see every movie that hits the theaters? Do you consume a lot of fast food? Some costs cannot be cut, but take a look at where your money is going and consider getting rid of expenses that aren't vital. You can also contact certain creditors and companies and tell them you've had a financial hardship; they may agree to spread out or defer your payments for a brief time.

4. Visit your campus financial aid office. Many colleges have emergency grants and scholarships for students in this type of situation. Do not hesitate to ask them as soon as necessary. You might also consider reaching out to the specific college or department your program is affiliated with. Similar to the financial aid office, some of these places offer relief grants or donations.

5. Talk to your professors. I've said it before and I am going to say it again: You need to stay in touch with your professors. Is your financial burden a dead car with no other way to get to school? Ask about temporarily working via e-mail. Do you have a sick spouse or child

in the hospital? Please tell your professors—they may not be able to help financially, but they can at least accommodate your workload to ease your anxiety and stress during such a difficult time.

6. Visit the career center. If you lost your job, head over to the career center. They can help you find a new job, prepare for interviews, and write/improve your resume.

Sometimes the only option is to take a break from school, and that's okay too. Keeping your family safe and healthy is your number one priority. School will still be there once you get back on your feet so don't let a financial burden be the reason you leave forever.

Failing a Class

Right from the start I'm going to tell you that failing or taking a break from college does not make you a failure. I've come to realize that most of us moms in college are major overachievers. We drive ourselves to the brink of exhaustion and then feel terrible when we fail. The many challenges we face in college, both inside and outside the classroom, teach us something—even if that lesson isn't part of the class description. If you're failing a class or fear you might fail, take heart—it happens to many students and isn't the end of the world.

First of all, many colleges allow you to retake a class in order to achieve a better (passing) grade. Once you pass the class you failed, the previous grade will remain on your transcript but will no longer affect your GPA. I know even this can seem disheartening, but I encourage you to remember that every failure teaches us something. You might learn to schedule your time better or you may find a better, more effective way to study. Sometimes a particular class isn't a good fit for you. You might realize that calculus isn't your thing, or a particular foreign language requires too much time for your circumstances. Whatever the problem, failing a class is not the end of the world, nor does it make YOU a failure. Rather, it makes you human. Do not base your worth on passing or failing one class. Here are some things you can do:

Be proactive: When you realize you can't handle a class, don't throw up your hands and wait for the end, hoping the Grade Fairy will wave a magic wand and grant you a C. Take action to prevent an F on your transcript.

Talk to your academic counselor. You need to know what impact this grade will have on your overall plan. For example, you won't be able to take the next class in a series if you fail the first one. You may need to rearrange the next semester's schedule and register again for this class. You might need to take a summer class to stay on track for graduation. Be honest with your advisor and for her advice.

Before you fail, ask for an Incomplete: Some colleges will let a professor give you an Incomplete, but this is usually granted circumstances, such as illness or a death in the immediate family. And, to qualify for this, you'll need a passing grade before you stop attending class. If something extreme happens in your life that leads you to believe you can't finish a class with a passing grade, speak with the instructor before you begin failing and give him a proposal for finishing your work later.

Analyze why you failed. Did you goof off too much? Over-commit yourself to other activities? Fail to study enough for exams? Turn in late, or incomplete, assignments? Was your professor an issue? Deciding what went wrong will help you understand how to pass the course and prevent further failing grades.

Consider withdrawal: Sometimes you can withdraw from a class, although there is a deadline for this (usually within the first month of a class). Withdrawal gives you a clean slate with no failing grade. If you keep your other grades up, later you may be able to get a retroactive withdrawal that will remove a failing grade from your transcript. Talk to your academic counselor about the options.

Retake the class: When you're feeling low about a failing grade, take action. If your failed class is a requirement, consider retaking it with the same professor. At least you'll know what to expect. If you had issues with that professor, take the class with a different instructor, but let that person know what happened. Be honest and discuss the areas you had trouble with. Ask the new professor for advice.

Taking a Break from School

Sometimes you need to defer your college education to focus on things that are happening in your life. This is not an easy decision, but may be your only choice. The good news is—it happens all the time, and you *can* return to finish your education. I am here to tell you that taking a break is not the end of the road for you. Just be sure to speak to an academic adviser and to someone in the admissions office. You don't want to have any loose ends when you're ready to come back. You might consider easing back into college with online courses. Before you leave, make a return to school plan with your advisor.

I can't list every issue that might take you away from college because almost anything can happen. Just this semester I had the stomach flu, morning sickness, one jaundiced child, and another with bronchitis—all in one week. All kinds of issues happen to student mothers like us. Just remember, this isn't about reaching the finish line first—it's about getting your degree with the knowledge that you didn't give up: you endured, you came back, you overcame adversity, you learned something valuable, and you took it all in stride.

Earn a certificate while you're out

Many community colleges offer eight week courses in over 30 different career fields, including healthcare and human services, advanced automation, biotechnology, design technology, and more. Earning a short-term certificate in your chosen field can lead to employment that will not only help pay the bills, but also give you experience that may lead to a better job after you return to school and graduate. Some employers will help with tuition if you're a good employee.

Don't feel guilty about taking a break from school. Recent studies show that more and more traditional students are taking a "gap year" away from college. Enjoy your time away from school, save money, hang out with your kids, and appreciate what you have in life. Colleges want you to graduate, so when you're ready to come back you may be surprised by how helpful your advisors will be. During your time off, continue reading about your interests and major subject. Sign up for online forums, local groups, and volunteer work. Stay focused and don't lose sight of your ultimate goal—a college degree.

Chapter 10

Celebrate Your Success

RHONDA

> "The look on your children's faces and the pride you feel will make all your struggles worthwhile in the end."

LIZ

> "Today I am 47 years old, a mom with self-confidence. I believe in myself and no longer doubt my ability to continue my education and make a difference in my community."

TO MOST PEOPLE, success in college is defined by graduating with a degree or professional certificate. That is only partially true. Along the way, as a mom in college, you will experience success in many different forms. Whenever you finish a class, complete a semester, make a good grade, or finally get a degree, you've accomplished something. In fact, just showing up every day is an accomplishment. I challenge you to step up and own every tear, late night, and missed class because your kids are vomiting. Own every year you were "still" a student, and every setback you overcame. Those moments brought you to this moment. This moment belongs to you—embrace it.

A College Degree

Obtaining your degree is a major success! You've earned at least 65 units and spent more time in class than in your own bed. You turned in the assignments, wrote papers, overcame math anxiety, worked on the dreaded group projects, drank your weight in coffee, passed the exams, and conquered speech class. You then focused on your major and delved into the subject, probably learning more than you ever expected. Earning a degree takes a lot of commitment and I know it feels great to hold that piece of paper in your hands—so hold it high!

Training for a Career

Most of us returned to school in order to learn enough skills to find a real career. That's true for me, at least. Over the course of your college career you'll learn specific career-centered skills defined by your major, and you also learn soft skills. Soft skills aren't always described on the syllabus because they come through experience. These include oral and written communication skills, leadership, teamwork and collaboration, adaptability, problem solving, and interpersonal skills, to name a few. When you successfully train for a career, you gained these skills also. Now you're ready to enter the job market as a competitive applicant, thus improving your income and living situation.

Cultural Awareness

For me, one of the unexpected benefits of college was becoming part of a diverse community of students. I learned so much about other cultures and became less ignorant about issues like race, class, and gender identity. I also become more aware of issues we need to help fix in our world. As a college student you'll be exposed to culture through your classes, clubs, events on campus, internships, jobs, study groups, and just hanging out in the student lounge. Learning to understand

and appreciate our peers regardless of race, class, gender, or religion is one way in which we become better people. If you can do this, your college experience will further enrich your life. College successfully helps us more fully understand all facets of life—the good, the bad, injustice, beauty, and how other people manage to overcome adversity.

Self-awareness

Through your college experience you'll gain knowledge and understanding about your own values, beliefs, desires, work ethic, feelings, and place in the community. You might even learn where you need to improve in those areas. You'll become aware of how you react to stress and adversity, how you handle success, and your attitudes toward different ideas and ways of life. Being self-aware takes a lot of blood, sweat, and tears, but if you work hard to improve yourself, you can celebrate this success, too.

Confidence

Lack of confidence is a common issue for moms in college. Chances are you walked into your first college class feeling like a lost, awkward mom-person. Perhaps you thought others found your presence bothersome or unusual, and maybe you doubted you could ever finish college. Now, after overcoming every obstacle in your path, you've grown into a confident scholar who's ready to take the next step. You know you can succeed because you've done it over and over through individual classes, whole semesters, entire academic years, and major projects. You can walk away from this part of your life with confidence, knowing you earned every single second of your success—and you can do it again in the next stage of life.

Grit

There's a chance you've heard this word quite a bit lately. Grit has become a topic of conversation, especially among the education community, but what is it? The Merriam-Webster Dictionary defines grit as "firmness of mind or spirit: unyielding courage in the face of hardship." Other definitions talk about the texture of stones. Imagine if you will, that a stone has been tossed around and ground over and over until it became smooth and lovely to look at. Grit is the stone's ability to adapt to that process. The same can be said for you. You've been through a lot of gritty processes such as failing, lacking confidence, feeling guilty, struggling to balance life and school, etc. Yet, you've proven you have grit. You're able to make it through difficult situations without breaking. Your tenacity has made you gritty.

Leading Your Children

I wanted to save this for last because, while all the other successes are important, this is the one thing I'll always be appreciative of and thankful for. As a mom in college, you have the potential to change the lives of your children in many, many ways. Most important is the fact that you will eventually improve your financial situation, giving your children a better chance to succeed. Second, you've been a shining example of what a successful student should look like—how a good student should act, and why it's important not to give up. Your children have seen you struggle with homework, study for countless hours, fail and bounce back, and overcome difficult issues both in and out of school without quitting. You've become a leader for your children, which is something that can never be taken away from you, or them. You should be proud of yourself, because although they may be too young to acknowledge it now, they will eventually express their pride in you.

Each of us defines success in a different way, and it can encompass much more than I've listed here. In many ways, college gave me opportunities to improve myself and the lives of my children. I've become an advocate for myself and my family, seeking out opportunities instead of waiting for them to come to me. I hope that as you finish this book and your college experience, you'll look back and realize just how successful you have been.

Chapter 11

Taking the Next Step

ANITA

> *"Although I had many economic and personal struggles, I graduated with an Associate's Degree in Humanities. I then transferred to Cal Poly Pomona University where I graduated with a Bachelor of Arts degree. I'm excited to say I'm now in the Master of Arts in English program at Cal State Fullerton. As a 22 year old, I never envisioned I could make it this far. In the end, what makes the difference is not just having a dream, but having the courage and patience to believe it can be real. Envision what you want for yourself and go get it!"*

YOU'VE OVERCOME MANY obstacles in your academic life, connected with professors and peers, and done your best to succeed in college. What's left? That depends on you. Your next step might be:

- Transferring to a four-year school.
- Starting graduate school.
- Preparing for licensing exams before starting your career.
- Finding a job if your education is complete.
- Taking a break from college with the intent of returning later.

1. **Transferring to a four-year school after community college.**

If you've decided to continue your education in a four-year school, congratulations! Most community colleges have transfer agreements with universities. These are the questions you should ask at a community college before you apply:

- Does this school have a special transfer relationship (often called an articulation agreement) with any four year colleges?

- What is your graduation rate for enrolled students?

- How does the school assist students in finding employment after graduation?

- Will the credits I earn be accepted at the four year colleges I'd like to consider?

- What grades do I need to earn in order to credit at four year colleges?

- What's the minimum GPA I need to maintain in order to transfer?

The first two rules in transferring are: Start early, and make a plan. You should initiate this process near the beginning of your last year in community college.   Many community colleges have partnerships with nearby universities to make transitioning smooth and easy. Choosing the transfer university should be a process whereby you ask for advice, research the best schools for your major, and determine the ideal fit for you. Speak with your academic counselors and your favorite professors. Be aware that unaccredited colleges can steal your finances, wreck your academic life, and take advantage of students who don't have mentors.

If you're uncertain about your goals, share your confusion with a professor or counselor and ask for advice. Ask your professors about their academic choices and strategies. Share your financial concerns and ask what scholarships are available, as well as when you should apply (the sooner the better, in most cases). While professors may not be familiar with updated financial aid or loan regulations, they will often give you great advice about investing in your potential and being smart about how you invest your money in education and your future.

When you do transfer, you'll start as a junior if enough of your courses are accepted. If you don't get credit for a particular class you may need to take it over at the four year college. When you graduate from the new school, only that college's name will appear on your bachelor's degree.

Once I started attending the university, the scariest part wasn't about being the new kid. Instead, I felt a bit of culture shock. At a community college it's much easier to run into other nontraditional students, but it took me a while to find "my people" when I transferred. That doesn't mean you won't meet other moms at the university; they're just harder to find in the sea of students. Once you get used to the campus you'll love exploring the options available at a larger school. Here are the most basic steps for transferring.

1. **Choose a major (if you haven't already).** Choosing a major is essential to transferring, and the earlier the better. If you haven't already decided go back to Chapter 6 and weigh your options.

2. **Research schools.** I imagine you'll search within a 20-mile radius of your home because of your situation. Being a mom in college reduces our options (most times) as far as school choices, but don't let it limit you too much. Consider the benefits and drawbacks of your community college and make a list of what you MUST have in a school.

3. **Visit the transfer center.** Your school probably has a transfer center that will assist you with the process. They have a wealth of knowledge on transferring, so please take advantage of that. They can also help with other

application procedures, such as personal statements. Furthermore, they will assess your academic credits and see what will be accepted.

4. **Visit the schools you're interested in.** I recommend visiting all the universities or colleges you'd like to attend. Your transfer center will likely have a list of upcoming tours, so take advantage of those opportunities. Someone familiar with the campus will walk you around and show you the campus, a great way to get to know the school. You can also make an appointment with the academic advisor in your chosen major, allowing yourself a look inside the department. Whatever you do, don't choose a school without stepping on campus first; you want to make sure it's a good fit.

5. **Apply!** But don't just apply to one school. Even if you have a 4.0 GPA, you shouldn't consider only one school. I was fortunate to get into my number one school, but I applied to five, just in case. The last thing you want is to apply to only a single college and not get accepted, delaying your transfer date to the next semester. Once you complete your application you can send transcripts. Make sure you apply to both the school AND the program you want for your specific major. Getting admitted to a university doesn't always mean you're automatically admitted to a specific program, such as nursing. You'll need to complete those application materials also—and the deadlines may be different. Research this and stay on top of it.

6. **Wait.** This is my least favorite part of anything concerning academics. Some schools will assign an identification number and e-mail address as a way to keep the lines of communication open before they accept you. If so, you'll have access to the status of your application as well as a list of items the school would

like you to submit, such as transcripts. Once you do that you'll have to wait while decisions are made. This time can range from weeks to months, depending on the school. However, you probably won't hear anything until after the application period ends, so check on that date to set yourself at ease for a while.

7. **Appeal.** If for some reason you don't get into a school you felt you were qualified for, don't be afraid to appeal the decision. Sometimes this happens and the best thing you can do is advocate for yourself. Contact the particular school and find out what needs to be done. You might win the appeal and you might not, but it doesn't hurt to try.

8. **Say "Yes/No" when you know.** As soon as you know what school you prefer, accept your admission and say no elsewhere. That way a spot will open for students who are on the waiting list.

Transferring to a larger school can be a scary transition, but it's one of the best choices I made concerning my college career. While it took a while for me to feel like part of the new school, soon enough it became my new home.

2. **Starting graduate school.**

If you're now ready to graduate from a university, you may want to consider grad school. Back when I began classes at a community college I would've laughed if someone told me someday I'd be taking graduate courses. But here I am, anxiously awaiting my acceptance letters to grad school. If you need to obtain a master's degree or higher, then graduate school will be your next step.

Obtaining a job is also usually part of this step, because most graduate students work during the day and attend school in the evening, which is why you'll find classes scheduled in the evening to accommodate working people. I like this because it means I can be with my younger children for a large portion of the day and even take the older ones to school, something I missed while working on my undergraduate coursework.

So why go? Well, you may need to in order to get the career you desire. For example, I want to teach college English, so I need at least a master's degree in order to teach at a community college. Many fields have this requirement, so be sure to investigate career paths for your degree in order to plan ahead. Additionally, a master's degree can mean a higher salary, depending on your field and the relevance of your specific degree. Above all, earning this degree will truly help you improve as a person.

The process for applying isn't much different than applying to college or transferring. You need to obtain a few letters of recommendation, include some type of work sample (writing for me, as I'm an English major), and possibly take the GRE (graduate record examination). These are common requirements along with the normal application, but I encourage you to research your desired school/department and find their exact requirements so you don't miss anything before the deadline.

Graduate school is a different world from undergraduate studies. I recommend speaking with professors about the program and, if possible, talk with a student who's completing the program. If you can find an alumnus, ask to meet with that person and go over the pros and cons of the program, including the career path. This will give you a better sense of what to expect in the coming one to two years of your education.

You may even plan on obtaining a Ph.D., which will take a year or two longer. If you start doubting your abilities, think about how far you've already come. I can tell you I have fear about receiving a doctorate because that sneaky imposter syndrome gives me anxiety. I start questioning if I'll ever know enough to write a dissertation. However, I do know this: By the time you're ready to write a dissertation, you ARE an expert in your field. Not only that, but writing the dissertation is a learning experience. It may take a full year, but that's okay because you're spending that time expanding your ideas and knowledge, possibly conducting research, and allowing your project to grow into itself. Don't let the task at hand overwhelm you. Think of any major project in steps, not as a whole. Overall, when you finish your graduate studies (be it master's degree or Ph.D.) you will be proud of the work you accomplish.

3. **Preparing for exams before starting your career.**

If your career field requires you take a certification exam, now is the time to begin studying (if you haven't started already). Once again, the career center on campus is the place to go, as well as your department. Many departments offer test preparation that will help you do your best, and your school may even offer the exams on site. You can probably find practice tests online or at school.

Be sure to research the exam requirements before you finish school. If your school doesn't offer test preparation, they probably know where to look for a good program. Exam anxiety is a big issue for many people, since this seems make-or-break time for your new career. Remember, you can probably repeat the test if you fail—but I'm betting you won't fail! If you care enough to read this book, you're going to pass the first time. A few preparation tips:

- Consider starting a study group or find a study partner with whom to review the material.

- Take practice exams and note where you had problems. This is important.

- Plan a study schedule six months in advance. Start with the basic material you learned and work your way up. Or, divide the study time into different aspect of the overall material and study one part at a time.

- Create lists, diagrams, and flash cards of the main topics and things you need to memorize. Say them aloud, so you'll be learning by reading and by hearing. Practice controlling your anxiety with deep breaths. On the exam, you may encounter subtle questions that seem tricky. Don't panic. Stay calm and read slowly.

4.   **Finding a job if your education is complete.**

If you're in a field that doesn't require a bachelor's degree, it might be time to start looking for an open position to launch your career. In fact, you should begin looking for a job before you finish your community college degree. That's why college networking is so important. You may be competing with thousands of other new graduates, plus older people with experience who've been laid off. If you've already made contacts through internships, volunteer work, and networking with alumni from your school, you might land a job even before you graduate.

The Career Center on campus is a helpful place to visit. They can provide leads, interview tips and practice, as well as help with your newly minted resume. Even if you finish school with a 4.0 grade average, that doesn't guarantee a job. You need to mobilize early and be focused. Here are ten tips for finding a job:

1.   Internships and volunteer work are extremely helpful. They may not seem important now, but when you graduate you'll wish you'd done more.

2.   Try and find a mentor within a company—someone who's already doing what you want to do.

3.   Make friends in the school Career Center. Be a regular visitor.

4.   Network with everyone you know, including friends, family, church friends, and other acquaintances. Let them know what you're looking for and ask for help.

5.   Create a professional profile on LinkedIn.

6.   Don't just apply for jobs online. Get out of the house and drop in on employers. Attend conferences where you can meet people in your field

7. Know what you want to do. Have one or two target jobs, not a vague idea of taking any job. Put together a list of potential employers and then identify contacts at each place. Research those contact people and try to find a connection you can use.

8. Your resume and cover letter are crucial tools. Never use generic resumes and cover letters—tailor them to each job you apply for and seek help in making them perfect.

9. Having a college degree with no experience is a handicap, which is why internships and volunteering are so vital. It's never too late to volunteer, and that may lead to a job offer.

10. If you have no job experience for your resume, think about personal traits and soft skills, such as friendliness, professionalism, and ability to follow through. Think how your Mom-skills can translate into job skills. The cover letter is crucial here, because you can explain why you'd excel at the job and why you're truly excited about the opportunity. Do not rehash the contents of your resume or use generic filler in your cover letter

Taking a break from college with the intent of returning.

If you're at the end of your bachelor's degree but aren't sure what you want to do, don't feel alone. Many people take a break after undergraduate coursework before continuing to graduate school or other training. This doesn't make you a quitter; it means you need to enjoy your life without the extra stress—especially as a mom in college. Take time to relish the duties of motherhood and don't feel bad about it. Personally, I won't take a break because I'm afraid I'll never return to finish school, and I hear that often from other mothers. However, I also know several moms who finished college and were eager to return after a break. It may be just what you need.

Whatever choice you make, remember it is *your* choice. You're the one who has to endure whatever your next step is, so be sure to make the choices you feel are best for you and your family. No one knows your goals as well as you do and they certainly don't know how much you can handle. You've already proven to yourself that you're capable of achieving success at every stage of this journey, and I applaud you for it. Now, it's time to decide on the next step!

I'd love to have you follow my blog **College Success for Moms** at https://collegesuccessformoms.wordpress.com/.

Chapter 12

Moms Like Us

THIS IS YOUR book. For several years I've worked on this material and considered all the possible issues you might face as a mom in college. I'm aware of the fact that, despite the challenges I overcame as a low-income mother, I am privileged. I understand you may not relate to me because of age, ethnicity, or marital status. If that's the case, then this chapter is especially for you, because it's dedicated to diversity among moms attending college. Each of the stories I've heard from other women inspired me with their grace, tenacity, compassion, and grit. That's why I want to share these stories with you. I hope they'll help you feel less alone as you travel through your academic journey.

Liz

School has always been my safe place. Childhood held more than a few challenges for me, including adapting to a new country, the death of my beloved father when I was nine, and my stepmother's untreated schizophrenia that resulted in neglect and abuse after my father died. Compared to my chaotic home life, school became my haven, especially as I began high school. But by the time I entered senior year, my stepmother's erratic behavior resulted in extended absences from school as I tried to care for her. In desperation, I dropped out of high school at the beginning of my senior year, only to enroll at the alternative high school two months later where a family friend taught. Based on my test scores and work there, the guidance counselor encouraged me to enroll at a different high school where I graduated a few months later.

Needless to say my grades were abysmal, my student activity record was sporadic, and none of the colleges I wanted to attend would even think of accepting me. I decided on a program at the local community college. Not long after the semester began my stepmother's condition became unmanageable. My grades plummeted, I was a nervous wreck, and I eventually dropped my classes to follow my stepmother as she moved from one state to another. At each stop I tried to take a few classes. Usually I was successful, sometimes not.

A few moves later I found myself in upstate New York attending my fourth community college and felt I was finally on track to finishing my degree. My grades were good, I loved my professors, and had even figured out a career path. And then I met my future husband six weeks before he was set to deploy to a support base for what would be known as Operation Desert Storm. Eight months later I packed my bags to begin life as a military spouse. By the age of 28, I was the parent of a son with a chronic, disabling health condition and a daughter newly-diagnosed with autism. Not long after that I became the full-time caretaker to my husband who became disabled while serving in the Air Force. My dreams of completing my education were not just put on hold; they were shelved for good. In place of my dream I completely immersed myself in the world of special diets, advocacy, homeschooling, and caretaking for my family. These things consumed every minute of my life.

I never imagined I'd return to school at the age of 45, and this could have—maybe should have—been a disaster. I thought I was crazy for even thinking about going back to school and had plenty of good reasons not to even try. But with my husband disabled and my children soon aging out of their healthcare program, returning to work was the most sensible option. I knew a college degree would be a valuable asset as I searched for employment.

Aside from concerns about my husband, one of my biggest worries was how to fit classes around real life, including routine but irregularly scheduled appointments at the Veterans Administration hospital. One nearby college not only offered online classes, but degree options fully available online. While I hadn't previously thought about completing my entire degree program online, this definitely sounded like a plan that could work with my busy schedule. Still, I'd heard about the difficulties of taking classes online and the high rate of failure for students who took these classes.

I decided to test drive the idea of online classes by enrolling in one free online class. I figured if I could work my way up to the equivalent of fulltime coursework this way, while also juggling life, I might have a chance when college credit was on the line. This proved useful in more ways than I could imagine. I was able to figure out what worked, what didn't, pinpoint my educational strengths and weaknesses, and know when I was at my sharpest. I also learned I needed to schedule regular down time for my own sanity. As any caregiver knows, we don't have much leftover time in the day for ourselves, and there's little room for error when stretching oneself so thin. Like many caregivers I put the health of my family before my own health, so before I began attending classes for credit I needed to make sure this new life would be compatible with my COPD, lymphedema, and scariest of all for any student: my ADHD!

The life-saver for me was learning to break my studying into bite-size portions and get up to stretch and do something active at regular intervals. The activity could be anything— folding laundry, emptying the dishwasher, or even playing dancing or fitness video games—so long as it got me up for a few minutes so I could process what I'd just read.

Getting through college takes hard work and dedication, especially as a mom, and I certainly can't take full credit for my achievements. In large part, my success as a returning student was due to the programs and resources in place at my community college. Campus resources and the support of my children completely changed the game for me this time around, allowing me to graduate with two Associate in Arts degrees.

In many ways the last three years of college were better than a dream come true, but during this same time I also faced some of my greatest life challenges. Not long after I reentered college, my best friend passed away suddenly from a heart attack; her death left me reeling and feeling lost. Though we lived an ocean away from one another, she too had recently returned to college and we made a pact to finish together. At the same time it became obvious that my marriage was unsalvageable. My husband had never been supportive of me having a life or interests apart from being his wife and caretaker. While he was interested in the financial potential college might reap, he wasn't at all inclined to support me in my studies. Without the initial and ongoing support of my children I would never have completed my first associate's degree; they helped me hold myself together when it felt like our world was falling apart. My son Christian and daughter Kat made great sacrifices and took over the majority of the housework to make sure I had time for coursework. They have been my most dedicated cheerleaders throughout this journey. They were there to quiz me on my study material, make meals, clean the house, and help take care of their father and our family ranch. During the years when their friends spent extended time away from home with friends and outside activities, Christian and Kat chose to take on greater responsibilities at home to help me reach my dream of finishing college.

If my children were the foundation of my support team, my professors and the college staff and administration served as the framework for my success. From the first semester my professors offered support, encouragement, and pointed to resources that would help me stay on track and succeed. Even though I took online classes, most of my professors were engaged and active online, and took time to send emails and leave helpful discussion responses and feedback on written assignments. My most frustrating class during my first semester was Introduction to Psychology; there was so much material to cover and learn and I repeatedly doubted myself. I felt old, out of practice, and like I couldn't keep up with my classmates. My professor, who also served as director of the college's counseling program, was incredibly positive and offered something invaluable: belief in me. At the end of the semester she wrote a note telling me one of her greatest rewards as a professor came from being a resource to her students. She reminded me to keep in touch with her. Almost two years later when my marriage had finally exploded, she helped me receive counseling, connected me with my first job in over 20 years, and has been so much more than just a professor.

My Women's Studies professor and Women's History professor, who also was director of the Women's Studies program, were also instrumental in my success. My Women's History professor saw I was earning top grades, but grades from my first attempt at college were pulling my grade point average down. She encouraged me to seek academic forgiveness for my previous poor performance which brought my GPA up enough to qualify for scholarships. She also included me in the yearly Women's Leadership Conference, including assigning an honors project to be presented there. Thanks to her support, I placed as a top five winner in the Women's Leadership Conference Scholarship competition.

My philosophy professor patiently guided me through the honors program which allowed me to graduate from my college with honors. Three wonderful literature professors taught me the value of accepting constructive criticism with their humorous and kind critiques. Because of the support and encouragement of my professors, I continued through each semester even when I wanted to give up.

College staff members and administration helped to connect me with resources, including tutoring and scholarships offered by my college and within the community. At every level the staff and administration reach out to help students. The Director of Graduation Services worked with our Phi Theta Kappa chapter and encouraged me to submit a scholarship application for a national organization that awards scholarships at the state level. Thanks to his support, I placed first in my state for the scholarship. As any mom in college knows, finances are frequently a major source of stress and this helped alleviate one of my major issues. But he didn't just encourage me to submit the application—he called me while I was attending a Phi Theta Kappa convention to tell me the news personally— and he accompanied me and the second-place winner, also a student at my college, to the awards ceremony where we received our scholarships. The staff and administration served as daily support on the ground; when I wanted to give up, someone was always there to make me laugh, listen to me complain, and keep me facing in the right direction.

Campus organizations and clubs were a surprising source of support for me. While our college is small, they offer an amazing variety of clubs and activities to keep students engaged. I have been active in, or served as an officer in, the Non-Traditional Students Organization, the Hispanic Students Association, Bakeology (the campus baking club), and Survive and Thrive, a campus organization dedicated to raising awareness of domestic and intimate partner violence. Membership in Phi Theta Kappa International Honor Society was an extremely validating and educational experience. I received my invitation after I completed the Academic Forgiveness process and felt surprised that anyone other than me cared about how well I did in college.

Participation in Phi Theta Kappa was a driving force to keep me in college and helped build my confidence in myself and my abilities. My advisor encouraged me to run for office and her support helped me become chapter president. Thanks to her, I was named one of the top five officers in the region two years in a row and my advisor was named one of the top fifteen advisors in all of Phi Theta Kappa for 2016. Aside from this newfound confidence and faith in my own abilities, this experience taught me skills I had no idea I could master: teambuilding, conflict-management, planning on a large scale, creative thinking, innovation, public speaking, technical writing . . .the list could go on and on.

Campus activities helped me form one of my strongest support systems—friends and kindred spirits. Through my classes and campus activities I met mothers like me, mothers very unlike me, and other women who faced challenges in completing their degrees. I was honestly surprised to form such close bonds with my Phi Theta Kappa officer teammates; these men and women have become more than friends; we are a family who continued daily texts, emails, phone calls, and meetings long after our year of service was over. My dearest friend, who I met through college, is also a mom with similar concerns. She balances college with a full-time job, housework, care of an adult child with epilepsy, and a son in grade school. Her friendship kept me steady through frustrations, despair, and many a midterm.

My return to college didn't just affect me, it touched my entire family. I had no idea what this journey would entail or how much I would grow and change through this experience. Today I am 47, a mom with self-confidence. I believe in myself and no longer doubt my ability to continue my education and make a difference in my community. In May 2016, I graduated from my community college with Associate in Arts degrees in both psychology and women's studies. I am enrolled for fall semester at the state university to continue working toward a bachelor's degree in social work with a minor in gender studies. My experiences and success in college encouraged both of my children to enroll at the same community college, which gives me the chance to cheer them on. Both children have received the same amazing support from faculty and staff that I received. When my daughter was eight and still struggling with reading I came to accept that she might never attend college. Today she is a double major in computer networking and library science.

The semester following my return to college, my son decided to enroll as well. He is currently assistant editor of the college paper, an active officer in campus clubs, and a scholarship student. One of my proudest moments as a student and a mother was serving as chapter president on the same Phi Theta Kappa International Honor Society officer team as my son.

I am thankful beyond words to Christian and Kat who made enormous sacrifices and offered endless love and support so I could do this college thing. I know they will each be successful in their own college journeys. I'm also grateful for the incredible support and encouragement I received from the staff, administration, and faculty at my college; their encouragement helped me become a successful college student and directly influenced my decision to continue my education past the associate's level.

CHARLENE

 My name is Charlene Carmona. Before this year I was Charlene Delgado.

I first felt my love for the medical field at a young age. I would go visit family members while they were patients in a hospital and feel amazed by all that was going on. My uncle and aunt, knowing my curiosity, allowed me to tour the different floors of a hospital. I once saw a nurse attending to an elderly person with so much care that I knew I wanted to be just like her.

As time passed and I grew up, I wasn't sure what part of the medical field I wanted to be part of. Did I want to be a doctor or a nurse? My youngest brother was born when I was 18 years old, and I remember talking to the nurse who cared for my stepmother. She told me I was probably looking to be a nurse practitioner. I was hooked. So I finished high school and did my homework on what colleges would be best for me.

Life has a funny way of showing that the plans we make are not always the paths we take. My boyfriend asked me to marry him and I said yes. We were married shortly after my eighteenth birthday and still adjusting when I found the college I wanted to attend. I was excited about it and knew I would get there, but I needed his support. He was a soldier in the Army and after talking it over, I realized if I decided to go down the college road, it would have to be without him. He had to go where he was told. His career was already started and mine still a dream, so I made a not-so-hard decision at the time to focus on being his wife and supporting his career. I felt certain my day would come.

Years passed and we went from one child to three. At the same time, my husband's schedule became more demanding. Our lives were busy and my dream of becoming a nurse seemed a distant memory. I still wanted to help people and the desire to work in a hospital was still there, but my role as a mother and wife took top priority.

Twelve years into this life, everything turned upside down when my husband decided the life we built wasn't the one he wanted. He left for something new and I was left with three deeply hurt children who couldn't understand. I knew I wasn't making enough in retail to provide for my family, and after being left with nothing, I needed to take action. I decided having a career was a better option than just having a job. I visited a couple of colleges and found one where I could start. I felt nervous about enrolling because this was a major step and I didn't want to fail. Failing my kids has always been my greatest fear and I had so many doubts as I closed my eyes and signed my name. I chose night school so I could make sure my children were ready for bed before I left home. My first night was nerve wrecking, but as time went on, I loved school.

Month after month passed and I was on way to being a medical assistant. This was a hard journey for me. Every month was something new; a different class, a new teacher, and another personal problem. About halfway through the program I wanted to run for the door. My divorce had been filed and my soon to be ex-husband stopped helping with the kids and the bills. I felt like I was drowning. Dealing with a divorce while trying to take monthly midterms and final exams was a huge challenge. I thought long and hard about my next step: Should I go back to retail and make the money we desperately needed, or continue to better myself for the future?

I chose to stay and continue with college.

The day I was finished was the last day of my externship and I sat in my minivan and cried. I'd done it! In spite of everything going on and people trying to stop me, I crossed the finish line. A few months later when I walked across the stage, the feeling I had deep inside my soul was indescribable. I was shining bright and beaming with pride. I cried then too. Tears of joy rolled down my face as I crossed the stage while my name and achievements were read.

Every month had been a struggle. Every month I had doubts, but every month my name was on the Dean's List and I passed to the next class. I wore my honor cords with pride, but my tears were for more my children. I cried because I saw my family standing for me, cheering me on. Standing on the chairs so I could see them, were my children, all three of them with smiles on their small faces, clapping, and proud of me.

I didn't fail them because I didn't give up, and I plan on doing it again soon, because I still have a ways to go before I achieve nurse status. My advice to you is: Don't give up. Whatever obstacles come your way, keep going. You will stumble, you will fall, and you will sometimes feel it's too hard to stay on this path. Don't give in to what is easy. Keep striving, keep moving your feet. Pick yourself up, dust yourself off, and stick to the path. You only fail if you stop trying. The look on your children's faces and the pride you feel will make all your struggles worthwhile in the end.

BARBARA

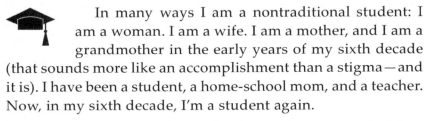 In many ways I am a nontraditional student: I am a woman. I am a wife. I am a mother, and I am a grandmother in the early years of my sixth decade (that sounds more like an accomplishment than a stigma—and it is). I have been a student, a home-school mom, and a teacher. Now, in my sixth decade, I'm a student again.

Choosing to go back to school wasn't an easy decision, especially at this time in my life. It was, in fact, daunting. I had so many questions: Could I do the work? Could I keep up with the young minds of the students who'd sit in classes with me? Should I go? What would be the purpose of getting an M. A. at my age? What would people think? Answering these questions caused me to face the fact that I was placing limits on myself. Fortunately, I have a loving, supportive family, and my grown children talked sense to me. They said they were sure I could do it, but the only way I'd know for sure was to try.

So I jumped into to the deep end, applied, and was accepted to the M. A. program. Now, as I write this, I'm getting ready to start my third and final year. In May I will graduate with an M. A. in English. Certainly I have learned a lot in my chosen field, but I also learned so much more.

An M. A. in English requires a lot of hard work. My first task was figuring out how to add school to my life. The things I did and the choices that I made may not work for everyone, and actually they shouldn't. Each of us must find her own path and figure out what does and does not work.

Before applying to school one of the first steps I took was having a talk with my family. This decision was mine, but it would affect all of us. While I knew I had their support, I wanted to talk about the changes that would happen and what they could mean. My husband has a saying, "The distance between expectations and reality is a gap filled with frustration." I wanted to give everyone a chance to verbalize their expectations and adjust them, so the reality of school wouldn't derail our lives. While this may seem old fashioned to many women today, because my husband and the children who still live at home are working busy jobs and in school, I was the one in our family responsible for most of the "house" work: shopping, cooking, and cleaning. For all of us, it was important for me to say out loud, "I'm going to be attending classes and studying. Sometimes I won't be home for dinner, and housework will have to be shared. We now have to share all these jobs." Setting these guidelines at the beginning really did help. My family responded by telling me they were all adults and would figure things out when I wasn't there.

The second thing I had to do may seem obvious, but for me it was a steep learning curve: I had to let them figure life out. I had to put down the guilt and not run to the rescue when they handled things at home in a way I didn't like or might have done differently.

Sometimes when I wasn't there to make dinner, or when I was busy with homework, these adults in my family chose to get take-out. Okay, that's reasonable. Sometimes they chose to dine on sandwiches, cereal, or even chips and salsa. Honestly this was harder on me than on them. All my "Oh, I'm a bad mom" guilt rose to the surface. But I learned. I learned that no one starved. I learned these people could eat a "non-dinner" of chips and salsa without perishing. I learned the dishes might not be washed the way I chose or when I would have chosen, and that was okay. Finding things after someone else put them away might become a game of hide and seek, but that too was okay.

Next, I had to face the fact that deciding to go to school was one thing, but doing school work was another. Forty years had passed since my last class, but I knew doing the work would require time and effort. That meant I had to evaluate my life and rearrange my priorities. First, I set up a study area — a place away from the TV where I could close the door on the world so I wouldn't be tempted by the "First I'll just . . ." monster. You know:

"First I'll just do the dishes, then I'll read my assignment."

"First I'll just put in a load of laundry."

"First I'll watch a little television to relax.

Then I had to figure out the best time to study. I'm a split between a morning dove and a night owl, so I began getting up a little earlier and making homework Job One. This took discipline, but that discipline paid off. I soon realized that reading could happen early, but if I had a paper to write I needed to wait until everyone's day ended and I had uninterrupted time. That often meant late nights. As I mentioned above, I'm not 20 years old. It was frustrating to realize it now takes me longer to recover from late night writing sessions. I had to plan ahead in order to write a paper, and that plan included modifying the next two days' schedules so I could go to bed earlier.

School is a big commitment and I had to set up my life in a way that made it work. I would never have just "found" the time. I had to put classes and homework on my schedule in ink. I had to be honest with myself about how I work, and about what might distract or derail my intentions to study.

Finally, I had to learn that what others thought of me wasn't nearly as important as what I thought of myself. I expected people to see me as "that grandma playing school." I was so wrong. I can honestly say I've been accepted with respect since day one. It seems I was the one with the narrow view of myself. Most of my classes are full of students about the same age as my children. Because I've been around longer, I bring a different perspective. Certainly I have views that are different since I have more years under my belt, but other students have different viewpoints because they come from another area of the country, or another country altogether. When class discussions happen, the field is leveled because we're all students in a learning environment. I found that our differences, our unique perspectives, and the individual challenges we face brought us together and helped us all have courage. Along with everyone else, I was expected to show up and bring my best every day. I grew enormously.

As a mother, grandmother, and wife in my 60's, earning a master's degree is challenging, but I see that life holds challenges at every stage. Attending college for the first time when I was young, single, and on my own wasn't easy. Life was also challenging when I got married and became a mother. Life was tough as my husband and I worked and raised four children. I realize I've always had to face and overcome challenges. Going to school highlighted one important thing to me: I am a learner. It seems funny that I only see that now, six decades into my life. It is a great lesson. And to anyone out there wondering if you can face the challenge of school I say, "YES! If I can do it, you can do it!"

RHONDA

 I graduated from high school in June of 1978, excited about going off to college in the fall. Little did I know this was the beginning of a 38-year journey. For the first part of my college adventure I attended a small Christian college in Illinois and lived in a dorm, just like millions of other high school graduates. The school I attended was on a trimester system, so I was able to take three semesters worth of work during the first year. My boyfriend (now husband) graduated from this same college during the spring of my first year, and after the year was over I returned home and went to work. I dropped out partly because I didn't have any clear direction I wanted to take in life for my career. Therefore, I didn't return to school but got a job making good money.

This went on for the next six years, during which time I got married, had one baby and, was pregnant with my second when we decided I should quit working and stay at home with the kids. This is my true calling: a stay at home mom. After my second child was born I considered college again and started taking classes at a local community college. I took general education classes because I still had no clear direction for a career choice. After one semester, my husband's job relocated us to Arizona. We were there for a few years and I looked into the state schools there, but found them too expensive. Once again I decided school wasn't a priority. I had a third child, and then we found ourselves moving back to California.

After a couple of years back in my home state, I again considered going back to school. I was working a part time job as a church secretary and had a good friend who said she'd take care of my kids while I attended classes. Once again I enrolled in classes at a state university. I felt strange being back in a classroom after so many years and was a little intimidated by the 18 to 22-year-old students. However, I settled in pretty well and enjoyed the classes. I considered pursuing a degree in nursing and made it through a couple of semesters. But, low and behold, we were moving again—this time to Michigan. After the move I started working full time and changed jobs a couple times until I landed a position at Michigan State University. This was wonderful, because as an employee I could take classes for free when I had time. After a few years in this position, my husband's job caused us to move again, back to California.

After another two years, I was determined to finish school and enrolled at a local community college. Now I was a forty-something among 18 years old students—very uncomfortable for me. After a semester I decided this wasn't something I wanted to do anymore. I had a good job and a good life—why did I need school? So I worked and changed jobs. After talking to a coworker about career options I considered medical coding, which seemed like a good fit for me. While looking into how I could train for this, I found a school with a certification program totally online. I started taking these classes and before long I was close to actually finishing all of the requirements for this program.

By that time, I'd been working at my job for almost ten years and my salary increase nicely over that time. I started looking at coding jobs and found I would have to take a large pay cut if I changed fields. Why would I do that? I took some time away from school and looked at other possibilities. I got all my transcripts together from six different colleges and sent them to the last school I attended online. I asked the advisor to evaluate and see if I could reach an Associate's degree with what I'd already taken. She looked over everything and told me there were two degrees I could choose from if I took a few additional more classes. I chose the degree that required me to take two more science classes, and in May of 2016 I graduated with an Associate of Arts degree.

My husband and children were thrilled and wanted to make a big deal out of this accomplishment. But I felt ridiculous for taking 38 years to get a two-year degree. I accumulated over 120 credits in college courses and have an AA degree to show for it. I wasn't going to do any of the graduation hoopla or bring any attention to the fact that I was graduating. But after talking to my niece and a good friend, both of whom went to college later in life, I decided to walk in my graduation ceremony.

For me graduating is an achievement that comes with mixed feelings. I'm glad I have a college degree, but I always feel like I need to qualify that by saying, "It's only an AA degree." I know I should be proud, and am I'm trying to be. My sweet husband looked up some stats just before my graduation ceremony. He said about 90% of people in the U.S. graduate from high school, but only 50% of them go on to graduate with an AA or higher degree. He really helped me feel proud of my accomplishment.

So, after 38 years, three grown children, several relocations, and six colleges—I am a college graduate. My advice to you is to never be afraid to dive in and try something new. If going to a brick-and-mortar school scares you, consider online courses. Don't hesitate to rely on your support people. My children all completed college before me and helped me learn to research and write papers in the digital age. When I started college, research was all done in the library with printed books.

ANITA

I've always been drawn to literature and writing and loved to read all of the time as a young girl, so I knew I'd major in English one day. My mom made sure I always did well in school and she steered me toward her vision of my future. The dominant figure in our family, she planned everything: our days, our lives, and our entire futures. We were dependent on her. However, when I was 16 and my brother was 14, our lives turned upside down when she suddenly passed away. Life kept spiraling downward for years after that; my father turned into a depressed, broken man and soon became an alcoholic. Instead of going to college as my mother planned for me, I got married to escape life at home at the age of eighteen, in 2002.

Unfortunately, this wasn't the happily ever after I hoped for. After I had my daughter at the age of twenty, my husband became emotionally and physically abusive. I had never met a person who could make me feel so bad, or who would do and say such terrible things. One of the things he liked to tell me was that I was "a waste of space, a waste of a brain, and a waste of air." I will never forget those words. I was so embarrassed and ashamed that I hid the physical abuse from family and friends; I covered my bruises and never told anyone what I was going through.

On July 4, 2005 I finally made the decision to leave him. I could no longer allow my daughter to grow up in a household filled with such negativity and abuse. When I told him I wanted a divorce and he held me captive in my room at knife-point for fourteen of the scariest hours of my life, until my brother called the police who only asked him to leave. I used this opportunity to escape with my daughter, and I purchased a bus ticket to Yuma, Arizona where my father had made arrangements for my cousin to pick me up and drive me to my godparent's home in Mexico. I stayed there for a while until I decided how to move forward.

When I came back reality was waiting, and I realized I was a twenty-two-year-old, divorced, single mom of an almost two-year-old little girl. From that point on I knew I had to be strong for both of us and press on, no matter how terrible I felt. I always told myself that, although I had a hard time believing it, I deserved a degree and a career just as much as anyone else. At this point I told myself I deserved the best, and I would go to school and get an education no matter how long it took.

Nevertheless, once I enrolled it was hard to focus on school; I took care of my dad and my daughter for years. I worked as a loan processor, a graveyard shift server, real estate transaction coordinator, and a manager throughout the years, all the while taking one or two classes. This was part of the reason I failed at the first community college I attended; my job was commission centered and I spent almost every waking moment at my office, from 8:00 in the morning until nine in the evening—hoping to make extra money. As a result, I put school aside. Then in 2008, the housing market began to crumble, as did my career in mortgages. I watched my dreams tumble down around me, and I went from making good money to almost no money. We lost most of our clients and the company closed. Just like that, the three years I devoted to this company were only a memory.

During that time I worked the graveyard shift as a server for almost a year; I worked till seven in the morning and all holidays and weekends. One day I realized my daughter was growing up fast and I was missing all of it because I was always exhausted. At that moment, I knew my daughter and I deserved more. I could never forget that year when I struggled so much—I would never let myself forget it. Despite having another stable job, in 2010 I made a resolution to attend school again.

However, it wasn't all smooth sailing from there. I would be entering school with a lot of emotional baggage because I didn't have the best track record at the first community college I attended, where my GPA was at a whopping 1.6. So I decided to begin my journey at a new college with a fresh start. I resolved to enroll at Mt. San Antonio College—the best decision I ever made.

I felt insecure when I first started at Mt. SAC. While I was confident in the business world, I hadn't succeeded in academia and that baggage kept me from participating in classes and asking questions. I was scared of feeling stupid. Also, my parents were Mexican immigrants who had only finished middle school. None of my immediate family members had attended a four-year university, so I had no one advising me on what steps to take. I should have been asking a TON of questions instead of being so prideful and inhibited.

In the fall of 2011, my whole life changed when I decided to take a British survey literature course with Dr. Betsy McCormick. When I entered her classroom, I couldn't have known the impact this fiery little woman would have on my life. When it came to writing for her class, I was lost. I hadn't written anything other than business emails for many years, and her expectations were extremely high. I received D grades on my first papers and was frustrated with myself—and often with her. She intimidated me because she was tough, blunt, and no-nonsense, which made me wonder if I could ever meet her expectations. I pushed myself constantly and worked hard on her papers, but oscillated between loving her class and almost quitting every week.

However, deep inside I felt if I could pass that class, I could do well in any course. I kept pushing and earned a C in her class as my final grade. Most people would have been upset with a C, but I couldn't have felt prouder. My sweat, tears, and frustration paid off, and after taking her class I would never get a C in a literature course (or any course) ever again.

Although I had many economic and personal struggles, I graduated from Mount San Antonio College in June 2013 with an Associate's Degree in Humanities. I then transferred to Cal Poly Pomona University where I graduated in June of 2015, at thirty-one years old, with my Bachelor of Arts degree in English Literature and Language and a minor in TESOL. I am excited to say I'm now in the Master of Arts in English program at Cal State University Fullerton, and I recently obtained a Teaching Associates position. By the end of spring, 2017 I will have completed my M.A. in English.

I'm also happy to report that my daughter is a self-assured and motivated twelve-year-old girl who attends a GATE academy and has her own dreams of success. Although my journey has been hard for both of us, I know that seeing me accomplish my goals has made her aspirations seem more attainable.

Additionally, I'm engaged to an amazing man who is wonderfully supportive of me, and I'm also blessed with a father who has been an amazing supporter of my academic career.

As a twenty-two-year-old, I never envisioned I could make it this far. What kept me going through it all? I realized that money comes and goes, employers can replace you with someone else, and some people will want to tear you down. But no one can ever take away what you've learned or how you feel about yourself. Yet, in order to move forward I had to change the way I saw myself. I could no longer focus on what I *should* have done, because I couldn't change my past. In fact, now I don't want to change my past because it made me into the person I am today. I finally stopped viewing my mistakes as huge failures and began to see every mistake as an opportunity for growth.

I still struggle every day to stay optimistic. To offset my doubts and fears, I maintain a close circle of friends who aspire to become better students and human beings. Everyone has their own personal demons, and that's why you should always surround yourself with people who want to see you succeed and who nurture your potential. In the end, what makes the difference is not just having a dream, but having the courage and patience to believe it can be real—and then taking small measures to make it happen: Envision what you want for yourself and go get it!

MELISSA

At the age of thirty-two, I made the decision to return to college for a B.A. in English. When I returned to Cal State Fullerton I was a wife, the mother of a four-year-old son and two-year-old daughter, and a full-time working professional. I was happy with my career and making a nice salary, but felt the yearning to complete my degree. Although I didn't need a college degree to advance in the workplace, this was a part of my life that felt incomplete.

I considered returning to school for quite some time, but waited until I finished nursing my daughter and felt she was old enough stay home with Dad for an extended period. This also meant talking to my husband about his changing role, as he would now become the primary caretaker for most of the week. I admit this scared me more than anything. I didn't want my husband resenting the fact that my priorities changed and he would suffer the consequences of my decision. He met the challenges that came with this change and still hasn't let me forget it! I actually enjoy his playful digs as a reminder of what a huge support he was. Having a supportive husband and a mother-in-law who jumped at the chance to help with the kids was the greatest blessing on my journey to graduation.

Another huge debt of gratitude is due my boss. Having to go to the president of the company and ask for an altered schedule wasn't easy for either of us. I didn't anticipate my education interfering with my work schedule; however, but I couldn't find online classes in my major, and only a few night courses. I voiced my desire to continue my education and he voiced his concerns about fairness in the workplace. In the end, a formal agreement was written up allowing me to take a salary cut in exchange for a thirty-two-hour workweek. My boss encouraged me, always checking to see how things were coming along. As a person who became a self-made millionaire with no college education, he was extremely supportive of my personal goals. Having his support meant a great deal to me and encouraged me to do well in my classes to make him proud.

Taking a cut in pay was relatively easy for our family because we became debt free about a year before I returned to school. The decision to live a debt free lifestyle allowed our family to still function through a 20% cut in my salary. As the main breadwinner for our home, this was a large chunk of our income. I was often envious of students who were able to quit their jobs, not work at all, or the like, but this wasn't financially possible for our family. I also used money I had saved to pay my tuition, allowing me to graduate debt free. Although this may not be an option for every student, I think working and keeping student loans as low as possible is something every student should consider, especially those with families.

For my first semester back I signed up to take five courses. This seemed like an insurmountable task, but I told myself I would at least try. The worst case scenario would be dropping a class or two. I know setting the bar high can add stress to returning to school, but I mitigated that by allowing myself grace if I couldn't meet the standards I set for myself. I had a plan for failure, and that's as important as a plan for success. I also told myself that even if I was failing a class I would still show up for every session, no matter what. This was important to me because I wasn't just attending classes for the grades—I felt like a dried up sponge dying to soak up knowledge. So, even if I couldn't keep up with the work I wanted to learn as much as possible.

I did feel nervous about was my age. Being a thirty-something woman in a sea of teenagers and young people who have yet to legally shotgun a beer didn't sound like fun to me. Adding to my discomfort was that on my very first day, in my very first class, as the professor walked in, I shrank in my seat wondering how much older I was than the professor. It turned out not to be the case, but I quickly understood there would be plenty of uncomfortable situations in my new experience, so I'd better get used to the feeling.

Through my first semester I awakened each morning at five, got myself and my kids ready (waking small children at 5:30am is awful), dropped my daughter off at grandma's by six, dropped my son off at pre-school on the way to the office, worked from seven until three (noon two days a week), headed to campus, and went to class until ten at night. Then I made the one-hour drive home, kept up on my reading until about midnight, and shuffled upstairs to peek at my sleeping children and plop into bed next to my slumbering husband, only to get five hours of sleep and do it all again the next day. I listened to as many audiobooks as possible in the car. I read during lunch breaks, bathroom breaks, and during the occasional web meeting (book held under the desk). I did not leave home all weekend because I used this time to do my homework. It was difficult watching my husband walk out the door with our kids to go to a party or see a movie, but this was the only time I had for homework and each minute was precious.

Many people asked me how I did it, and after first acknowledging my supportive husband, I often told myself, "It's only sixteen weeks." Keeping this perspective helped remind me that, although I often felt tortured and exhausted every day, sixteen weeks is a relatively short time. Anyone can do almost anything for sixteen weeks, and that's just what I did. Finding support through a journey like this is critical, but supporting yourself is paramount.

Part of supporting myself also meant seeking help when I needed it. I managed this in two important ways. First, I made appointments to see my professors during office hours when I needed help. As a younger student this was something I never did, always feeling a bit awkward about bothering my teachers when not in class. As an older student I found these meetings were critical to my success, and I no longer viewed my teachers as some sort of higher-level beings with whom I wasn't fit to share conversation. I kept in mind that I was paying their salaries and I wanted to get every penny's worth. Using this resource helped me do much better on assignments.

Secondly, I made a friend — a fellow college mom who knew the ins and outs of "college stuff" helped me out tremendously with the intangible things that neither I, nor my professors, could give me. She told me I could get equivalency for a class I dreaded taking the following semester, not to mention, also wreaking havoc on my schedule. She talked about assignments with me and often gave a different perspective and understanding that helped me gain deeper knowledge. Most importantly, she was me: a mom in college trying to do her best. Finding another mom I could look up to was something I didn't know I needed.

In order to complete my degree in the fall semester I took two classes over the summer. This wasn't easy or cheap, but allowed me to save on tuition in the long run because I was able to graduate by taking six classes, the most allowable, during my last semester. To many people this seemed impossible, but I did it while also achieving a 4.0 GPA. My point is: Every accomplishment I achieved seemed impossible, but I just did it. Sometimes things felt uncomfortable, scary, new, or completely foreign. I felt stupid sometimes, but I got through it. The thing with that is, often you aren't the only one with that same "stupid" question or feeling, and sometimes you just need to put yourself out there.

During my first semester back, on the first day of one of my classes, the professor told us to get our laptops out. There was no such thing as a laptop the last time I went to school. Needless to say, terror set in. "Crap! Now I have to bring a computer to school!" At the next session I brought a laptop, but terror crept in again when everyone around me started logging in. I had to ask my teenage neighbor how to log into the computer, all the while thinking, "Now he's going to tell all of his friends about the old lady he sat next to in class who didn't even know how to log in to the classroom computer."

This wasn't the first or last time I faced an uncomfortable situation, but after the first couple of times I stopped caring and realized how happy my fellow students were to help out. Everyone has their own struggles, so when it was my turn to help someone, I would jump at the opportunity.

One key to my success was the commitment to show up. On the days when I was exhausted, felt unprepared for class, or wanted to be somewhere else, I reminded myself of the one thing I committed to: Show up for class every single day, no matter what. Being in class contributes to student success in ways nothing else can. Hearing what your fellow students contribute helps your mind expand, and you learn so many things you might never think of on your own. Being present shows respect for the time your professor puts into preparing the class. Showing up assures you know the value of the hundreds, and thousands, of dollars you're spending on a service that will grow in worth exponentially throughout your lifetime.

I-Esha

 I always knew I wanted to be the type of mom my daughter could look up to. When her father and I separated, I felt devastated because this wasn't how I planned for things to work out and I felt I'd let her down. I had my daughter after I received my bachelor's degree, but I always wanted to go on for a post-baccalaureate degree. I knew relying on my ex wasn't a possibility as he didn't play a very active role in my daughter's life, so I relied on my family for help with childcare and moral support. I had no idea how tough the road was going to be, but I knew this was something I wanted to do. Going back to school while my daughter was young turned out to be the best decision I ever made.

Being a student with a child is a tough life at times. I felt there were few people in my situation. Most of my classmates were either married with children, older with grandchildren, or young with no children. I also hated leaving my child. When I decided to go back to school my daughter was about a year old and feared leaving her for long periods of time and missing out on things. I also feared my ability to handle the responsibilities of being a student and the duties of being a mom. I felt overwhelmed in the beginning and had a lot of self-doubt, but having my daughter motivated me to keep going. As the sole provider, my job was to secure our financial future—and more education would help me do that.

While finishing my bachelor's degree I decided to become a teacher for children with special needs. When I finished completing my credential program my daughter was four years old. I liked going back to school while she was young, because she got to see me study, do homework, and work toward my goals. School wasn't easy, and it was definitely a financial burden at times, but I'm now working my dream job and providing a good life for my daughter. I'm showing her she can do anything she sets her mind to. I actually plan on pursuing my doctorate degree in a few years.

I encourage any mom to go back to school, no matter the age of your child. You will set an example of hard work and the value of education. Do not let fear, doubt, or finances be the determining factor. Looking back over the years, I could have quit many times, but I stuck with it. My daughter is my constant motivator who keeps me striving to do better. I always say, "Education never gets old and never goes out of style."

DIANA

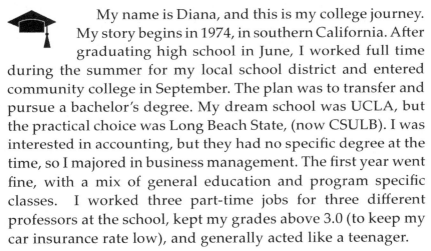 My name is Diana, and this is my college journey. My story begins in 1974, in southern California. After graduating high school in June, I worked full time during the summer for my local school district and entered community college in September. The plan was to transfer and pursue a bachelor's degree. My dream school was UCLA, but the practical choice was Long Beach State, (now CSULB). I was interested in accounting, but they had no specific degree at the time, so I majored in business management. The first year went fine, with a mix of general education and program specific classes. I worked three part-time jobs for three different professors at the school, kept my grades above 3.0 (to keep my car insurance rate low), and generally acted like a teenager.

During the fall of 1975, a friend from high school contacted me and we started hanging out. She fantasized about how great it was to be on your own, how much fun you could have, no parents telling you what to do, no curfews, no rules. At the time I was also getting advice that experience was more important than a degree, so with all this "great" advice, I dropped out of school, got a full-time job, and moved in with my friend. Sure we had no curfew and no parents, but being on my own meant huge responsibilities. I went from living at home and only paying my car insurance ($330 a year), to paying rent, utilities, buying food and sundries, and having to go to work every day, all day long. Yeah, oodles of fun. I tried taking a night class here and there, but it seemed as though my college dream had ended.

In 1984, I married and started my family. By 1992, I had two little girls in school full-time and decided to continue my college education. I took classes while the girls went to school and everything seemed to be working well, until I found out I was pregnant. This was a shock, since the doctor told me I wouldn't be able to conceive any more children. I finished the spring 1993 semester and put college on hold. In 1996, I returned to school at night, and in February 1997 my mother suffered a heart attack and again I found out I was pregnant. I decided this was a sign the Lord wanted me to devote time to my family, so once again I put everything else on the back burner.

Over the years my children grew and my husband's job took us to central California and then southern New Mexico. I was a full-time mom, a foster mom, worked at our local army base and did what was necessary for my family. In 2004, eight weeks after moving to New Mexico, away from all my family and friends, my husband was deployed to Iraq. A few months later my second oldest daughter moved back to California with her aunt. My oldest was in the Army stationed in Korea and I was alone with my two youngest children, ages eleven and seven. Money was tight, as our income had nearly been cut in half and there were times I had to depend on credit cards more than I wanted to.

After my husband returned home and we needed to pay off the debt we incurred over the past year and a half, I returned to the work force as a cafeteria worker. It was the only job I could get with basically the same hours and days the girls were in school. My oldest was out of the Army and had moved back home. She would get the girls to the bus in the morning and I was home before they returned from school. After the third daughter graduated and the youngest was in high school, I changed jobs and went to work at Walmart.

Finally, when I felt the girls were old enough—three out of high school and one almost there—I made the decision to quit my job and return to school full-time. I now had the time, the finances, (helped in part with the post 9-11 GI bill), and the desire to finish what I started. Forty years after I started college the first time, I returned to college in New Mexico. A different state, different degree plans, and different requirements, but nothing would stop me this time. Many of my previous college credits weren't accepted, so it was like starting all over again.

In the summer of 2014, I took a refresher course in accounting that didn't count toward anything other than giving me confidence in pursuing this degree. I also took an Excel class and earned an A. When I saw that GPA of 4.0, I decided my goal was not just to earn the degree, but also maintain a 4.0 average. Then came English. I tested high enough to skip the first two levels of the English requirement, but talk about lost! I hadn't taken an English class in forty years, and this one was taught on-line. Luckily I had a phenomenal teacher. She held several workshops for all of us to attend and two of my classmates were willing to get together and study. Unfortunately, the study sessions were on another campus an hour away, but it was worth the drive to get the assistance. The semester ended with my GPA intact.

The following semester I enrolled in an economics class. Two weeks before the semester started it was changed from face-to-face to on-line. Oh, no, not again! Economics is one of those things you love or hate. My instructor was passionate about economics; me, not so much. It took a lot of extra studying, research, and sleepless nights, but I survived.

My final semester arrived and I was almost there, feeling both excited and sad. I enjoyed the professors, my classmates, and the entire nerve racking experience, which was almost over. Then came BMGT 140, Business Management II, and the instructor was a no nonsense, mature woman, who pulled no punches and didn't want to hear any excuses. The first day of class she set the tone: "Get your syllabus on-line. You're responsible for knowing everything on that syllabus." She was the instructor, not our mom. She would lecture on the first six chapters of the book, and then each student chose a chapter or half a chapter and made a presentation. Fellow classmates graded how well you performed, and your grade was based on their assessment. My first thoughts were, "There goes my 4.0, my sanity and maybe this entire dream." I was wrong, wrong, wrong. She turned out to be one of my favorite instructors, a fascinating woman who has been around the world and visited or lived in every one of the 50 states. My first impression of her was right, but I didn't realize how much I'd like her.

So my journey spanned forty years, exactly, from the time I should have graduated in 1976. In May of 2016, I finally walked across a stage, shook hands with a college president, and earned my associate's degree. Although the people who would've been watching from the stands in 1976 were watching from a different arena, my husband, children, and granddaughter were with me to share the night. I accomplished this in two years and maintained that 4.0 GPA. I earned my way to the Dean's List, the Dean's Honor List, was a Crimson Scholar, and a Meritorious Graduate. I don't say this to toot my own horn—I say it this as encouragement to for you to never give up.

I want you to set goals and work hard to achieve them. So many times I wanted to give up and call it quits. After my first year I wondered, "Why am I doing this?" Then I ran into my algebra instructor at the grocery store and he told me how he used my story during the following semester to encourage a student to stay in school. She was struggling with being an older student and didn't think she was would be any good. He told her I said the same things, but turned out to be his best student that semester.

CECILE

 My name is Cecile Ann (Nicholls) Sinclair. My journey into the world of college began in September 1973, which was 43 years ago. I had big dreams. As a little girl I wanted to become a CPA. In 1978, I did the marriage thing and then went on to become a mother to four wonderful children: Jennifer, Jessica, Jon, and Jayme. They have been my inspiration to continue attending college throughout many struggles that included divorce, financial issues, and several serious health conditions.

After being married for about five years and giving birth to my second child, Jessica, I wanted to continue with school, but didn't actually follow that dream for quite some time after. After my youngest child Jayme, graduated from high school I finally enrolled in college again, after visiting the financial aid department at Long Beach City College. We didn't know it at the time, but because I was going through chemo therapy and radiation for breast cancer and no longer working, and my husband, at the time, was unemployed, Jayme qualified for aid—and so did I. So I decided that summer, in 2009, that I'd would go back to school and finish my AA degree in accounting. Since I was still undergoing treatments for cancer, I chose to enroll in online classes.

About a year and a half into school, my now ex-husband, decided he wanted to end our 30+ years of marriage. So, onward we went: We sold our home, moved to a new place, and I returned to school again, all the while looking for a job to help with rent. After I started working again, I realized the online courses were still the most convenient. However, in February 2011, my rent increased too much, so I moved back to my childhood home in Long Beach to live with my mother.

This is where my life took another turn. After surviving cancer and divorce I decided, with the help of one of my best friends, I needed to cross something off my bucket list. So, I moved to Port Orchard, Washington, in 2011, to live with my best friend and her family. What an exciting time. I enrolled in Olympic College in Bremerton, Washington, again taking online courses that were accepted at Long Beach City College toward my degree in accounting. Eventually I moved back to

Long Beach after being home sick and missing my kids, but the experience was worth it.

My life changed yet again on Memorial Day Weekend 2015, when I awakened with a terrible case of vertigo. I'd experienced vertigo once before, but nothing like this. After three trips to the ER and one trip to my new primary physician, they determined I had a reoccurrence of Meniere's disease, which I first had diagnosed back in 2012, when it caused me to lose about 90% of the hearing in my left ear. This bout of vertigo caused me to lose ALL hearing in my right ear and more in my left. I had about four to six percent hearing in my left ear. This condition also caused my left arm and leg to weaken and my right arm and leg to feel heavy. Now I use a walker when outside and can only drive short distances as long as someone is with me in the car.

During this difficult time I found out through my son in law that Long Beach City College has a Disabled Students Program and Services Department. I'll be the first to admit I'd never heard of this. When you don't have these issues, you don't pay attention to the services. This program and the department help with priority registration, registration assistance, disability-related academics, vocational, and personal counseling, on/off campus liaison and referrals, special orientation to campus facilities and programs, adaptive educational equipment (hearing devices, which did not work for me, but we tried), and materials and supplies. I received many benefits through DSPS, specifically a captioner (like a court reporter) who comes to class with me and takes notes and/or helps me communicate with the professor and other students.

With only a few classes left to complete, I'm excited about graduating in April, 2017. I've worked for many years to finally earn this degree. I survived so many challenges to get where I am today, and graduation will be my finish line. My advice to you is: Don't let disabilities, setbacks, and other challenges interfere with earning an education, regardless of what degree or certification you're seeking. Go for it!

TAMIKA

 I always expected to attend and graduate from college. I prepared for the experience for as long as I can remember by taking honors courses in high school and surrounding myself with like-minded people. School has always been easy for me. The biggest challenge for me was deciding between becoming an accountant or a brain surgeon.

In 1991, during my junior year of high school, I became pregnant. Life as I knew it changed. I was no longer a teenager planning for college; I was a teenager preparing for motherhood. My dreams for attending college were not crushed, just deferred. I always knew I would go to college. It was not a matter of "if" I would go; it was a matter of "when." From the moment I found out I was going to be a mom, I based every decision on how it would impact my child's well-being. Without hesitation or regret, I exchanged my teenage growth and development years for diapers and night feedings—the best decision I ever made.

In September of 1992, I gave birth to my daughter and made a vow to be the best parent possible. I felt responsible not only for bringing her into the world, but also for raising her to be her best self. I wanted her to be better than me. I wanted to teach her not to duplicate my mistakes in life, but to learn and grow from them.

Fast forward to 2009, my daughter's senior year of high school. With the help of a good friend I made the decision to enroll full-time at Citrus College. My initial decision was to wait until my daughter graduated from high school because then I would have fulfilled my obligations to her. But during her senior year she was busy with senior activities, AP courses, and college applications, so my role as her mother was changing. She didn't need me as much. Soon she'd go out into the world and make her own decisions. As she began her senior year of high school, I too began a new chapter in my life; my first year of college. My journey was just beginning. I had so many questions, including:

- How would I adjust to being surrounded by teenagers?
- Would I find time to study and do homework?
- Would I still be able to be available for my daughter when she needed me?

I soon discovered most of the people in night school were older students returning to school for career advancement. I could devote only one day a week to homework, usually a weekend day, and I didn't have to sacrifice my parenting for school or vice versa. School didn't occupy as much time as I expected.

My daughter graduated from high school in June 2010, as I completed my first year of college. She would attend CSULA in the fall. I continued my education at Citrus College for the next two years with a double major: business management and behavioral sciences. I graduated in June 2012, with honors. I transferred to CSULA with my daughter—her idea. She majored in psychology on her journey to becoming a PA, and I double majored in business management and computer information systems. I was a regular on the dean's list and was inducted into the Beta Gamma Sigma Honor Society my senior year.

In June of 2015, my daughter and I graduated from CSULA together—an unforgettable experience. Traditionally, a parent attends a child's graduation as a guest in the audience. I had the honor and privilege of sitting right beside my daughter during the graduation ceremony. We crossed the stage to receive our diplomas together.

Attending college seventeen years after high school was first and foremost for self-fulfillment. Secondly, I wanted to teach my daughter to never give up on herself or on her dreams no matter what obstacles cross her path. I raised my daughter to be great in everything she does in life. How can I expect greatness from her if she hasn't been exposed to it at home? My role as her mother is to be my best self so she will be inspired to always be her best self.

My advice to you is this: Your life's journey is yours to explore. No matter what paths you choose to take in life, or what paths life chooses for you, remember that God is in control of your destiny. Keep striving for your dreams and desires even if life's challenges derail you from your chosen path. Life is too short to be filled with regret. Nothing is more gratifying than accomplishing a goal you set for yourself, no matter how big or small. Ignore the people in your life who try to tear you down and say you can't succeed. Let their negativity fuel your success.

Epilogue

TODAY, I AM *somebody*—and so are you. Yet, ten years ago I could only see myself a failure. If you feel that way now, you are SO mistaken. I want you to know that many, many women have taken this same journey and done amazing things. Unfortunately, we don't know much about them because our society doesn't appreciate their struggles and triumphs.

We all know the difficulties of being a college student. Add to that being a mom, a wife, an employee, and possibly a caregiver for aging parents—and you have a major challenge ahead of you. Don't for one second think your journey won't be worthy of praise. Every class you complete and every degree you earn is something to be proud of. YOU are remarkable.

I hope this book will help you. I want you to feel proud and secure enough to connect with other women in the same situation. You may not know any other moms in college or you may know several, but either way I hope you find a friend in me. I felt alone for most of my journey, wanting to be part of the college environment but not knowing how. I hope you won't feel that way.

Now that I'm further along in my journey, meeting other moms has become an incredibly uplifting experience. I find inspiration in each story I hear and I encourage you to reach out to other "moms like us." I encourage you to read and reread this book whenever you feel alone.

At this point in my college experience I've earned an Associate of Arts and a Bachelor of Arts. My Master of Arts is just eleven months away. I successfully completed these stages in my education with enthusiasm, tenacity, and hope. Whether you're halfway through your journey, nearing the end, or just starting, I want you to believe you're capable of success. Never be afraid to step outside your comfort zone and follow your dreams.

Being a mom is a tremendous blessing in life and your most important role, but please don't forget that you are still *you*. Don't forget your dreams are worth pursuing, your thoughts are valid, and you are a shining example for your children. This journey may not be easy, but it will always be worthwhile.

Resources and Links for Moms in College

- **www.collegesuccessformoms.com** College Success for Moms, the blog. I blog often, come visit!
- **https://fafsa.ed.gov** Free Application for Federal Student Aid, the most important form you will fill out annually in order to receive funds.
- **http://ope.ed.gov/accreditation/** U.S. Department of Education Database of Accredited Postsecondary Institutions and Programs.
- **https://www.collegeboard.org/** The College Board online, a not-for-profit organization that connects students to colleges and offers many resources, including a step-by-step college search process.
- **http://pearsonstudents.com** Pearson Students—a website and blog devoted to students.
- **http://www.educationdepartment.org/daycare.php** Need childcare? Here is a list of colleges that offer childcare on campus.
- **http://www.bestcolleges.com/features/students-with-children/** Want to find a mom-friendly college? This site includes not only childcare, but other important factors like class meeting times.
- **www.fastweb.com, www.salliemae.com, and www.collegefish.org** (mainly for PTK students): all

great sources for scholarship opportunities outside of your college/university.

- **https://owl.english.purdue.edu/owl/section/6/23/** Need help writing a resume, personal statement, or CV? Look no further! The Purdue O.W.L. is there for you.

Books

Community College Success: How to Finish with Friends, Scholarships, and the Career of Your Dreams, by Isa Adney. NorLights Press, 2014.

College Success: Networking from College to Career, by Jarom Schmidt, MHSA. NorLights Press, 2015.

Index

Acknowledgements

THANKING EVERYONE WOULD require at least twenty pages, but I will do my best in one page to say a special thank you to:

- Mary Becerra for mentoring me through the first draft and allowing me to follow my passion and dreams. And thanks for the enchiladas.

- The CSUF Adult Re-Entry and WoMen's Center, English department, and Honors Program.

- Betsy, Ellen, Lana, and Marty.

- Mt. San Antonio College and Cal State Fullerton.

- Phi Theta Kappa—the best honor society in existence!

- Allison Jones, Kara Manis, and Isa Adney.

- Pearson, Pearson Students, and the absolutely amazing Andrea Shaw.

- Barbara Meyer for reading this book when it was in shambles!

- My family, especially my husband, mom, and Aunt Rhonda; you all encouraged and supported me and that made the difference between success and failure.

- And to my GoFundMe heroes:

Andrea Gatdula, Carolyn Koehler, Laura Coaty, Janet Duker, Laureen DeShay, Cristina Fiorentino, Lesly Gregory, Kristen Hallberg Hodge, Levena Lindahl, Gillian Seely, Beth Hyer, Simmy Ogg, Tracy Augustine, Dj Cannon, Sierra Sampson, Marianna Tu, William Black, John Wannemacher, Alexandria Pipitone, Anita Reyes, Kelechi Ikegwu, Taylor Bell, Melanie Kesler, Zeeshan Abdullah, and Margena Holmes.

About the Author

Dianna Blake

DIANNA BLAKE IS a mother, wife, student, and mentor. She is also a freelance editor and has worked closely with Pearson Students for the last three years while also attending California State University, Fullerton (CSUF). She graduated with her Bachelor of Arts in English in 2015 and continued at CSUF for graduate school. She is currently in her second year of the MA in English program, teaching English 101 and preparing to write her thesis. She will graduate in 2018.

As a first generation college student in her mid-twenties, Dianna began her educational journey at Mt. San Antonio College in 2007. She went on to win the Phi Theta Kappa "All California Academic Team" award and is a proud Alumni of the honor society. Now, Dianna works with various groups of students on and off her college campus, mentoring those who seek help. Outside of school and career, Dianna enjoys spending time with her family, reading, watching sappy romantic comedies, and going to church.

While this is Dianna's first book, she has published over 100 blogs at Collegesuccessformoms.com and for Pearson.

Made in the USA
Las Vegas, NV
26 April 2021